THE COSMIC RACE

A Bilingual Edition

Race in the Americas

Robert Reid-Pharr, Series Editor

THE COSMIC RACE:

A BILINGUAL EDITION

José Vasconcelos

Translated and Annotated by Didier T. Jaén

Afterword by Joseba Gabilondo

The Johns Hopkins University Press
Baltimore and London

First Spanish edition published 1925, © Herederos de José Vasconcelos. Bilingual
edition originally published by the Department of Chicano Studies, California State
University, Los Angeles, 1979.
Johns Hopkins Paperbacks edition, 1997
06 05 04 03 02 01 00 99 98 97   5 4 3 2 1

The Johns Hopkins University Press
2715 North Charles Street
Baltimore, Maryland 21218-4319
The Johns Hopkins Press Ltd., London

Library of Congress Cataloging-in-Publication Data

Vasconcelos, José, 1881–1959.
    [Raza cósmica.   English]
    The cosmic race : a bilingual edition / José Vasconcelos ;
translated and annotated by Didier T. Jaén; afterword by Joseba Gabilondo —
Johns Hopkins paperbacks ed.
        p.   cm. — (Race in the Americas)
    Originally published: The cosmic race ; La raza cósmica. Los Angeles : Centro de
Publicaciones, California State University, 1979.
    Includes bibliographical references.
    ISBN 0-8018-5655-8 (pbk. : alk. paper)
    1. Cosmology.   2. Evolution.   3. Race relations.   4. Philosophical
anthropology.   I. Jaén, Didier Tisdel.   II. Title.   III. Series.
BD512.V3713   1997
305.8—dc21
                                                                97-2484
                                                                CIP

A catalog record for this book is available from the British Library.

By 1650, New Spain already had some one-hundred-and-sixty thousand half castes or mestizos; they outnumbered the Spaniards. The castas *bred faster than Europeans and survived better than* indios. *Their population curve was rising sharply against those of other races. Slowly, painfully, and almost unnoticed, the* castes *were growing . . .*

T. R. Fehrenbach, *Fire and Blood* (New York) 1973, p. 263

CONTENTS

INTRODUCTION

I

The thought of the future has been a particular preoccupation of Latin American writers, but it was especially so during the first part of the XX century. Two essays of that period stand out prominently even today: Rodo's *Ariel* (1900), with its vision of a spiritually uplifted humanity, in contrast to the materialistic world of Caliban, and José Vasconcelos' *La raza cósmica* (1925), with a vision of the future Aesthetic Era of mankind.

In this essay, Vasconcelos predicted the emergence of a new age in the development of humanity. He called it the Spiritual or Aesthetic Era, in contrast with the Intellectual or Political Era in which we find ourselves at present, and the Materialistic or Warring Era which preceded it.

In our present age, reason prevails. Political and social groups are organized according to the logic of mutual convenience and reasonable exchange, or at least, that is the goal. Morals are supposedly ruled by ethical reason, freedom is regulated by laws of political expediency, and religions become organized institutions.

In the coming age, which even in 1925, according to Vasconcelos, was beginning to announce itself in many ways, all these barriers and regulations of the present age will fall away under the predominance, not of reason or intellect, but of creative imagination and fantasy. There will be no norms to regulate conduct, since actions will be based on feeling, dictated by the pathos of aesthetic emotion; or rather the norm will be given by that joy which is the outcome of the perception of beauty. Men will do their desire as directed by taste, not by necessity, appetite, or reason. Joy, love, and fantasy, that is, creativity, will be the predominant ingredients of human life.

As this age gradually emerges from the present dominance of reason, sexual unions will cease to be founded on necessity or on norms of convenience for society, since men and women will be guided by the free choice of love, beauty, and joy. Such unions will be more like works of art rather than the social contracts our present marriages are, and their offspring will be beautiful children of love and joy. Ethnic barriers will lose their force, and the mixture of the races, already in progress, will increase to the point that a new, fully mixed race will emerge, in which the better qualities of all the previous races will survive by the natural selection of love. This new race, in which all the present races will become diffused and eventually disappear, and which will be gifted with the power of creative fantasy over reason, is what Vasconcelos appropriately called "the Cosmic Race." Its universal dominance will coincide with the Spiritual or Aesthetic Era of mankind.

Whether the Cosmic Race will produce the Esthetic Age, or vice versa, is not clear. Perhaps the two will fashion each other gradually as they develop. However, since Latin America seems more advanced than other cultural areas in the process of racial mixture and acceptance of all races, Vasconcelos saw here the opportunity for Latin America to grasp the lead, by becoming aware of such a possibility and by deliberately working towards that goal in the development of Humanity. Vasconcelos' essay, then, is an appeal to the Latin American people to take conscious hold of this destiny which history and culture have put in their hands. Vasconcelos warns, however, that if Latin Americans lose their way by imitating the predominant Intellectual cultures and do not take the lead, some other culture will take their place, for nothing will stop the emergence of the new age which is already under way.

This, in summary, although perhaps not in this order of emphasis, is the thesis of Vasconcelos' essay *La raza cósmica*. Vasconcelos seemed emphatically to regard such mixing of the races, or *mestizaje*, especially as it is given in Latin America, as the fundamental requirement for the emergence of the new age. This led to unfortunate misinterpretations of his book, both by friend and foe. His essay has traditionally been taken as a racist theory for the encouragement of a people with deeply rooted feelings of inferiority. Such interpretation eventually caused the dismissal of his work as just another selfserving dream of the Latin American poetic mind. And although Vasconcelos denied that this was the intention of his essay, his own style undermined his protestations. Another shortcoming of the essay turned out to be its pseudo-factual or pseudo-scientific style, which led many critics to discuss his ideas from the point of view of science, especially from the field of genetics and evolution.

However, Vasconcelos' mind was not scientific, not even logical or rationalistic. Although his many works were an attempt to write a monumental philosophical system encompassing all mental human endeavor—art, science, religion and philosophy—the basis for it is intuitional. Thus, to reject his thesis only from the point of view of science and genetics is somewhat unjustified. Most critics who have done so, reject his ideas about "mestizaje" and, of course, the idea of a superior Latin American or Hispanic (even if Cosmic) race. But this idea of a superior Latin American or Hispanic race was not in Vasconcelos' thesis. On the other hand, his prediction of a new age for humanity goes, not only unchallenged, but suspiciously ignored. How can one bring up scientific arguments to reject a utopian fantasy? Vasconcelos' essay is obviously not scientific, it is divinatory and inspirational, and thus should it be read.

It is interesting, however, that theories similar to Vasconcelos' were later proposed by a more methodical and scientific mind. Such is the case of the French anthropologist Father Pierre Teilhard de Chardin (1881-1955). In *Phenomenon of Man* (written in 1935 but not published until 1955), Teilhard de Chardin proposes an awe-inspiring conception of evolution as a movement from a Material State preceding Life to the appearance of Life, then of Thought, and ultimately directing itself towards an emergent level of fusion within a divine entity. His books, banished from publication by the Jesuit hierarchy, seem recent, since they were not published until after his death. However, most of his writings belong to the decades of the twenties and the thirties, the period between the two World Wars and after. It is perhaps not surprising then, that there is a definite resemblance of aim, and even of ideas, between this writer and his somewhat forgotten contemporary, the Mexican Jose Vasconcelos. Both were products of that period at the turn of the century which saw a reaction against Darwin's and Spencer's purely biological and materialistic concepts of evolution. According to Spencer, evolution takes place in three stages: Inorganic, Organic, and Superorganic; respectively characterized by the absence of life, the appearance of life, and the final emergence of thought and social organization as the result of the development of the nervous system. This scheme is similar to that of Teilhard de Chardin's, but Spencer's evolutionary theory follows purely mechanical laws and is hence fatalistic and without direction. Opposing this, Henri Bergson, in his work, *Creative Evolution* (1907), proposed the theory that evolution is initiated and carried forward by a vital impulse. This *élan vital* is not mechanical but free and creative, therefore, unpredictable. Bergson's theory shifts the driving force of evolution from the purely materialistic and mechanical to the spiritual and free, but this force remains directionless, having no fixed beginning and making its own way as it goes. Theories like that of Teilhard de Chardin's (and Vasconcelos'), on the other hand, tried to assign a fixed goal to the process, thus giving it meaning and direction.

The similarity between Teilhard de Chardin's and Vasconcelos' views about race is even more striking. Teilhard de Chardin's views were expressed in an essay titled, "The Natural Units of Humanity, An Attempt to Outline a Racial Biology and Morality."[1] In this essay, concerned with the emergence of the new nationalisms and divergent demands of different racial groups, Teilhard de Chardin advanced the hypothesis of what he calls "the confluence of human branches":

> Beyond all doubt, humanity's advance, measured by an increase of power and consciousness, took place in fixed and limited regions of the earth. Historically certain ethnical groups showed themselves more progressive than others, and formed the advanced wing of humanity. Now to what factors do we suppose these groups owed their superiority. Qualities of 'blood' and mind? The best of economic resources and climatic conditions? Yes, no doubt. But we can also see that the sites of human development always appear to coincide with the points of meeting and anastomosis of several 'nervures' [That is, the points of mixture of different branches of the human 'species']. The most vigorous human branches are by no means those in which some isolation has preserved the purest genes; but those, on the contrary, in which the richest interfecundation has taken place. Compare only the Pacific and the Mediterranean as they were a century ago. *The most humanized human collectivities always appear in the last resort, to be the product not of segregation but of synthesis* (p. 206-7, underlined on text).

This hypothesis, based on his own interpretation of the theory of evolution, lead Teilhard de Chardin to propose the foundation of an international or interracial, that is, universal morality, which will aid the process of synthesis rather than hinder it:

To admit, in fact that a combination of races and peoples is
the event biologically awaited for the new and higher extension of consciousness to take place on earth, is at the same
time to define, in its principal lines and internal dynamism,
the thing that our action stands most in need of: an international ethic (p. 211).

Such theories strongly resemble Vasconcelos' ideas in his prologue to
the 1948 edition of *La raza cósmica*. Teilhard de Chardin was a Jesuit, as
well as a scientist of mystical and theological inclinations, who has been
described as "one of the century's most remarkable prophetic thinkers,
an Aquinas of the atomic era."[2] It is perhaps, then, not purely coinciden-
tal that Vasconcelos who was also attempting a Thomistic synthesis for
the XX century, should have, in the last years of his life, rejoined the
Catholic faith of his childhood under the influence of Jesuit friends. This
unpardonable (in the eyes of his anticlerical compatriots) and apparently
contradictory decision can be explained, perhaps, by an underground
affinity. Something in the Jesuit or Catholic vision tends towards unity,
even if sometimes, unfortunately, at the expense of individual freedom.
Vasconcelos, whose outlook leaned towards mysticism, saw a basic
opposition between individual materialism, centered on the self, and the
goal of universal unity, of moving towards the Self, thus he chose to
return to Catholicism interpreted in this light. We see in his whole life and
work a desire, and yet a failure, an all too human failure, to pass beyond
this diversity of self and Self. His faith in Catholicism and the Hispanic
tradition were expressions of that desire.

It is not quite fashionable to praise Vasconcelos in Mexico these days.
Any mention of his name brings recollections of his *Breve historia de
México*. His exaltation of Catholicism and the conquest was taken as a
personal insult by the Mexican intellectual elite — the product of an
emergent middle class which seemed to look for its roots only in the
Indian past and in the Revolution of 1910. On the other hand, his ideas
were summarily dismissed by the Marxists, perhaps with reason, since
what Vasconcelos proposed went, of course, beyond the reach of any
materialistic doctrine. Vasconcelos was then judged as a resentful politi-
cian, embittered by his defeat as a presidential candidate in the elections
of 1929, and as one of the most negative and pessimistic mentalities of
Mexico.

It is true that Vasconcelos, in his later years, became negative and pessimistic about the future of the Mexican nation, but his was the voice of one who felt that the Revolution of 1910 had been betrayed. Clearly, Vasconcelos' concept of the goal of the Mexican Revolution was not the transformation of Mexico into a new materialistic state, emulator of the technological development of the United States, and guided by the incentive of the dollar and personal comfort. Neither the capitalist materialism of the United States, nor the communist materialism of Russia was the model to follow. Vasconcelos, and a few others, thought that Mexico was taking a new road with the Revolution, a new direction, which nevertheless was born from its Catholic and spiritual past, and directed itself towards a future whose primordial goal was the total development of man, not only of his socio-economic and biological aspects. On this new road, Mexico would march at the vanguard of all other nations which would follow her guide, tired as they were of an economic materialism that lacked human dimensions. Economic materialism and utilitarian capitalism sought no more than the goals of ants, as had been already pointed out by Rodó in his essay written at the turn of the century:

> A definitely organized society which limits its idea of civilization to the accumulation of abundant elements of prosperity, and its idea of justice to their equitable distribution among its associates, will make of the cities it inhabits nothing different, in essence, to the anthill or the beehive.[3]

Vasconcelos and his associates sought another dimension for man and society, and this was the opportunity they saw in the Mexican Revolution. This vision explains Vasconcelos' action as Minister of Education in the development of the arts and public schools, in the popularization of the classics, and in the motto of the National University: "Por mi raza hablará el espíritu" ("The Spirit shall speak through my race"). This also explains his disappointment with a political development that moved away from that direction in order to concentrate merely on technological progress or personal ambition. But the Mexican Revolution followed the course imposed by the history and fabric of the Mexican nation. Vasconcelos was also part of that fabric and, as such, he found support in many sectors. But these intellectual factions were not politically the strongest (they seldom are in the history of nations, much less in a society born of the Positivism of the end of the XIX century). Although Positivism itself produced this minority that reacted against it, it also produced widespread aspirations at the economic and social level, aspirations that answered to the vital needs of the emergent masses. "Order and progress" the motto of Positivism, did not cease to be the motto of Mexican society after the Revolution. What the Revolution did was to change the basis of that order and to widen the field of social progress. This still is, for the most part, the aspiration of the governing classes. Nor was Vasconcelos opposed to that motto either, only that "progress" for Vasconcelos reached beyond economic welfare: Order and progress were not ends in themselves, but the basis for an ideal future development. The Mexican Revolution was not betrayed, Vasconcelos confused his concept of the Revolution with the reality of the Mexican Revolution. The latter triumphed and gave the results that were possible within its context and socio-economic aspirations. The other revolution is still to come. Vasconcelos was simply ahead of his times, as all visionaries are. Mexicans who remember only his *Breve historia*, and ignore the message of *La raza cósmica* commit an injustice, not only against Vasconcelos, but against their own history and future development, because the Aesthetic Era that Vasconcelos predicted is nothing less than an era of the expansion of human consciousness beyond the present limits prescribed by science and logic. The basis for this future development are integration and synthesis: Integration and synthesis of human personality at the individual level, of social classes and ethnic groups at the social and political levels. Marxism and "Vasconcelism" were not really too far apart, but Vasconcelos feared that social integration would be considered as an end in itself (that of simply increasing the material comfort of the masses, rather than the total expansion of human capacity), while Marxists feared an elitist development of the Revolution.

But visionaries are difficult to ignore when their visions respond to vital impulses of mankind. Recently, from unexpected quarters, Vasconcelos' name again acquired the aura of a prophet and precursor, and his concept of the Cosmic race has been seen again with more than passing interest; this, outside the political boundaries of Mexico, although within her cultural orbit. Some members of the Chicano movement in the southwest of the United States saw, in the early days of the movement, an exaltation of their own values in this concept of the Cosmic race, and identified with it the concept of "La Raza," giving it new life, when in

Latin America this concept had already been forgotten and had lost prestige.[4] It is not strange that this should be so. In the United States, the problem of racial and ethnic differences is still as vital as it was in the rest of the world during the first part of the XX century, when Vasconcelos wrote his book. Although Vasconcelos denied that his essay was written in order to exalt a race with strong feelings of inferiority, the tone of his work, and the interpretation it has received since it was written, contradicts him. Now, with the awakening of Chicano consciousness, Vasconcelos' essay offered the Chicano the same possibility of exaltation that it offered the Mexicans and the rest of Latin America when it first appeared. Nor is it arbitrary for Chicanos to include Vasconcelos as one of their own, since he lived the Chicano experience while attending school in Eagle Pass, Texas, when his father was customs inspector in Piedras Negras, Mexico, across the Rio Grande. "My experience in the school of Eagle Pass was bitter" — recalls Vasconcelos — "There I saw North American and Mexican children seated before a teacher whose language I did not understand." (*O.C.*, 1, 305).[5]

What does the "Cosmic race" mean to Chicanos? In some cases, it appears as a concept vaguely equivalent to the concept of "La Raza" but with a sense of the future: It is the triumphant "raza." For others, however, "la raza cósmica" is the universal race, the race of the future, as explained by Vasconcelos: The race in which all other races disappear. Yet, this idea is somewhat associated with the idea of the survival of the "Chicano." As if "La Raza" (that is, the Chicano) already were the Cosmic race, that is, the race that for its qualities of mixture or *mestizaje* had already acquired the vitality to survive and overcome all other races. It is true that *mestizaje* is one of the central concepts of the Vasconcelos essay, but, of course, it is also clear that the racial mixture Vasconcelos refers to is much wider, much more encompassing, than what can be understood by the *mestizaje* of the Mexican or Chicano, which is basically the product of only two races. But even if we expand the concept of *mestizaje* to include all other races, this biological mixture would not fulfill what Vasconcelos expresses with the idea of the Cosmic race, any more than a mixture of different breeds of chicken would produce a Cosmic chicken. The other part of Vasconcelos' concept, expressed in the adjective, *cosmic*, may have a nice sound to Chicano ears (and to other readers, as well), but remains with a meaning similar to the volutes of smoke and dust that in Azuela's novel, *Los de abajo*, rise from the violent field of the Revolution, embrace each other, unite, and finally

xvi

dissolve into nothing. At most, it is an adjective that produces mysterious echoes in the soul of the movement, there is something poetic about it and, therefore, it appeals. What is said here about the meaning of the concept of the Cosmic race for the Chicano, could have been said also of the Latin American public which received the essay with unquestionably ethnic enthusiasm in 1925, and again in 1948. As Gabriella de Beer notes, the theory of the Cosmic race "in its day fell upon very receptive ears and had great appeal for those people of mixed racial stock."[6] This does not mean, however, that some readers have not read other implications in the work. It is these other readings that account for the permanence of a work whose obvious ethnic theories would readily lose their attraction when confronted with scientific data or mere reality.

But not only among the general public does this identification of the concept of the Cosmic race with its biological implications occur. Vasconcelos himself contributed to that interpretation by emphasizing the idea of racial mixture or *mestizaje* in his later writings. He even reached the point of almost rejecting his own work when, confronted with the social and political reality of his own country and other racially mixed countries, he realized that the mestizo, only by the fact of being a mestizo, that is, a biological hybrid, is not necessarily going to reach the high levels of human development presupposed by the concept of the Cosmic race. Thus, Gabriella de Beer quotes from Vasconcelos' book, *El desastre* (1938): "...my own declaration of faith in mixed races resulted ironic to myself" (De Beer, op. cit., 302) and later she comments: "...in 1944, he publicly admitted that his theory of the emergence of the cosmic race in Latin America was a notorious mistake," (De Beer, op. cit., 313), although Vasconcelos is less firm, as he says: "quizás uno de mis yerros más notorios." Vasconcelos, in fact, does not seem to give up all hope for the future mixed race in his statement from *El desastre*, which quoted in full reads as follows: "With sadness, I returned to Paris to correct the proofs of my book *Indología*, in which the defense of colored races is made. After what I had seen in the Orient and the added evidence of that Congress [the Anti-imperialist congress held in Brussels in 1926] my own declaration of faith in mixed races resulted ironic to myself. Nevertheless, I approved the printing. *No doubt the time had not come, but it would come*. Cultures are not improvised, and it was necessary to continue strengthening the basis of a [cultural] flourishing that would give us the right to be free, by the proper use of freedom" (My underlining, *O.C.*, I, p. 1747). Other critics have also indicated an anti-Indianist

xvii

attitude in Vasconcelos and even characterize his whole work as anti-Indianist: "He finds no value at all in pre-colonial cultures; in an attitude similar to that of Sarmiento, he looks with disdain upon the mixture of races, and the mestizo must abandon his ancestry, his Indian roots, if he wants to survive the advance of progress..."[7]

It is not explained by these critics, however, how, after declaring that his concept of the Cosmic race was a "notorious mistake" in 1944, Vasconcelos would agree to publish a new edition of his work in 1948, adding a prologue in which he not only does not reject the book's theory, but tries to find new arguments to support it and to explain its apparent contradiction by Latin American reality.

De Beer interprets this prologue of 1948 as almost a negation of the theory. However, Vasconcelos qualifies his statements by suggesting that although the underdevelopment of the Latin American peoples, where the Indian element is predominant, is difficult to explain, perhaps it can be explained if we go back in time to the case of the Egyptian civilization, the product of a mixture of white and black races, an example cited by Vasconcelos in his prologue. Thus, he concludes, "it happens that the mixture of elements that are quite dissimilar takes a long time to mold" (p. 41 This ed.). This is very far from implying a rejection of the theory, instead it reveals an effort to explain those cases that do not seem to fit into it, and to support the theory that even the mixture of very dissimilar racial stocks produces beneficial results, given a considerable lapse of time, "of many centuries," he says, and he concludes, "as long as the *spiritual factor* contributes to raise them" (my emphasis, p. 3 this edition). This supports our contention that the theory of the Cosmic race is not simply biological. The spiritual factor, which during the conquest, according to Vasconcelos, "made the American Indians advance, in a matter of a few centuries, from cannibalism to a relatively civilized state," is what contributes the "Cosmic" element to the simple biological mixture of races. Such a spiritual factor was given to the Latin American conquest by Christianism and the Catholic Hispanic tradition, according to Vasconcelos. However, one should not confuse Christianity with the Catholic Church, nor the Hispanic tradition with the Spanish Empire, although both contributed to set the basis upon which, Vasconcelos believes, Latin America should build her future.

Perhaps then the main error in the interpretation of *La raza cósmica* is the tendency to consider this work from a strictly sociological point of view. This essay is usually classified with Vasconcelos' sociological works, and its ideas discussed from the point of view of genetics. On the other hand, many critics ignore the relationship of *La raza cósmica* to the philosophical writings of Vasconcelos, with which it forms a system that gives meaning, not only to his literary works, but also to his life, and even to his contradictions. As we shall see later, Vasconcelos was not attempting to write a scientific theory, since his basic philosophical attitude is anti-scientific, especially in matters dealing with the spirit.

A similar error occurs with the study and analysis of Vasconcelos' philosophical works from the point of view of traditional logic and philosophy. When his system attempts to be broader than traditional philosophy and science — not by rejecting them, but by encompassing them within a broader theory of knowledge — it is useless to apply to his writings attitudes and methods derived from such traditional fields. Perhaps Vasconcelos' mistake was to have written in a style that emulates science and philosophy, when he pretended to be more than a philosopher or a scientist. His problem was that of expressing in a rational language intuitions that surpassed the limits of language and reason. Where others wrote literature or created art, Vasconcelos tried to construct systems. His aim was that of encompassing within a complete philosophical system, such as Saint Thomas' the glimpses of a Nietzsche or a Schopenhauer, as well as the visions of science. Vasconcelos, in final analysis, gives the impression of a great intuitive mind which did not find its mode of expression.

Precisely in this titanic effort rests the permanence (as well as the weakness) of his work, because the idea of the Cosmic race, as the *Ariel* of Rodó, involves an intuition that is permanent, and an ideal which pertains not only to Latin America, but to the rest of the world as well. What Rodó and Vasconcelos saw was the possibility of reaching that ideal in Latin America earlier than in other lands, since the basis for such a future development was already present. They saw also the possibility that such a development could be thwarted by the influence of doctrines and attitudes predominant in the Western world, especially in the United States. *Ariel* and *La raza cósmica* were, thus, prophetic visions that sounded the alarm, but instead of predicting disasters and the destruction of old kingdoms, like Montezuma's priests, their visions searched for the light of a new dawn. Vasconcelos' essay, *La raza cósmica*, is an enduring testimony of a New World that is yet to come.

II

Before going into the essay itself, it is necessary to see it within the context of Vasconcelos' life and works. This in itself may contribute to clarify certain points.

Vasconcelos was born in Oaxaca in 1882, to parents of European ancestry (of Spanish, Italian and perhaps Sephardic blood)[8] not quite what Latin Americans call a *mestizo*. His early years, however, were spent in Piedras Negras, where his father was customs inspector on the Texas border across the Rio Grande from Eagle Pass. There, José attended grade school with Mexicans and Anglos, and had his first experience of the antagonism between the two cultures. But nationalist pride was overpowered by the fact that the schools in Eagle Pass were better, and his parents preferred to send him there, where he would have the opportunity to learn English. He was a promising student, and when his family had to move to Campeche in 1895, the school principal suggested that José remain behind to complete school and to be sent later to the University of Texas at Austin, where he could perhaps have studied philosophy and become a professor. This plan, however, was rejected by José (who had higher ambitions) and by his parents. Instead he went to the Escuela Preparatoria in Mexico City.

It was during these youthful years that some of the ideas that took a lifetime to develop began to emerge as Vasconcelos supplemented his studies with independent reading at the library of the Preparatoria and at the National Library. (This was a habit that continued throughout his life. When not involved in the political arena or in love affairs, Vasconcelos searched the calm corridors of whatever library was available — in New York, Washington, Austin, San Antonio or Berkeley. Wherever destiny took him, there was always the oasis of the library.) One of the early readings, Vasconcelos recalls, was the geographer Reclus' *Man and Earth:* "His statements about the living together of different races in America," says Vasconcelos, "were the germ of what I have later written on the subject." (*O.C.*, 1, 402.)

From the Preparatoria, Vasconcelos went to law school. His preference would have been to study philosophy, but the predominant ideology, Comtian Positivism, had eliminated philosophy from the curriculum and replaced it with sociology. Thus, his study of philosophy had to be carried on as an independent task.

Even before graduating from law school in 1905, Vasconcelos had begun his association with other young intellectuals, the novelist Martín Luis Guzmán, the philosopher Antonio Caso, the humanist Alfonso Reyes, and others, who, with the arrival of the Dominican Republic critic, Pedro Enríquez Ureña, founded in 1909 the Ateneo de La Juventud (the youth's forum). Their intention was merely to bring new ideas into Mexican intellectual life, but this resulted in their turning away from the predominant Positivism of the Porfirio Díaz regime, and more towards the spiritual renaissance of the turn of the century: The "vitalism" of Bergson and the idealism of Boutroux. Nature, according to Boutroux, did not submit completely to the reign of law; the underlying basis of the explanation of the world was the Spirit, which is free. This freedom is expressed in art, morality, and religion, which afford knowledge of a higher nature than scientific knowledge.

At one of the meetings of the Ateneo, Vasconcelos read his first philosophical essay: A study of Mexican Positivism and its main representative, Gabino Barreda. Vasconcelos recognized the contribution of the old intellectual to the development of Mexican education, but in the light of the new ideas, he rejected the old philosophy. Already at this early date, one of the basic ideas of *La raza cósmica,* the idea of the new Era of spiritual freedom, was hinted at on that occasion: "Freedom, which gradually has been taking us away from the domination of phenomenological laws, will tend to carry us even further each time, to the antithetical order, to the complete absence of finality, and will become *disinterest.*" (*O.C.,* 1, 52, underlined in text.) This intellectual and philosophical opposition to the Díaz regime was readily translated into political action for Vasconcelos when Francisco I. Madero invited him to help found the Anti-Reelectionist Party, later known as Partido Maderista, which opposed the reelection of Porfirio Díaz and proposed Madero as a candidate for the coming elections.

Even in these days, in the midst of all the intellectual and political fervor, the mystical thought of India had already caught the attention of Vasconcelos and his contemporaries. In his *Estudios indostánicos,* Vasconcelos recalls that it was in those meetings of the Ateneo de la Juventud that they began to read and be stimulated by Indian philosophy (*O.C.,* 111, 88.) and in the chapter devoted to the *Bahagavaad Gita,* he quotes extensively from Francisco I. Madero's commentaries on this Indian classic. Madero himself leaned strongly towards the mystical practices of

Spiritualism, of which he first learned in 1891 while studying in France, and apparently considered Vasconcelos a fellow Spiritualist.[9] Also during these years, Vasconcelos discovered and began to enjoy that other treasure of esoteric philosophy, Plotinus, and other philosophers of antiquity. "Poking into the exotic thought," he recalls, "at last I came upon my most permanent predilection: the School of Alexandria, which I met through the admirable book by Vacherot." (*O.C.*, 1, 542.)

Political participation as the editor of the anti-Díaz paper, *El Anti-Reeleccionista*, quickly led to persecution by the police and Vasconcelos fled on his first exile to New York (in 1910) where he found work as a translator of commercial letters. There, at the New York Public Library, he read and took copious notes on Indian philosophy, including the works of the Theosophists. (*O.C.*, 1, 611.) He returned to Mexico shortly afterwards, then left again, this time to San Antonio, Texas, to rejoin Madero in exile, and after Madero's triumph, returned to Mexico City again for a short while. After the assassination of Madero and a brief stay in prison, Vasconcelos exiled himself once more and went to Europe, where he traveled through France, Spain, Italy, and England. He returned to Mexico after the triumph of Carranza, in 1914, but broke off with him the following year and went back into exile in New York. There, he wrote his first philosophical book, *Pitágoras*, which was published in Havana in 1916. That year he also made his first journey to South America, where he worked in Lima for a while. In 1917, he went to San Diego, California, where, to support himself, he opened a law office. He completed the manuscript of *Estudios indostánicos*, and wrote his rather clumsy attempt at modern Greek tragedy, *Prometeo vencedor*. Both were published in Mexico City without difficulty. The basic ideas of *La raza cósmica* are already expressed in this latter work. One of the characters in the first act announces that in Latin America "Men of all races that have gathered there speak of forming a new humanity with the best of all cultures, harmonized and ennobled within the Spanish mold." (*O.C.*, I, 258). The new age is announced in the last act by the chorus: "This is the Aesthetic Era: Today no other law rules us except that of the intuition of a generous beauty." Then one of the characters explains: "We arrived at the Aesthetic Era, that is, the Era in which no end foreign to our own essence moves us, and our soul is free to follow the way of its better impulses . . ." (*O.C.*, I, 266).

Vasconcelos returned to Mexico in 1918, after the overthrow of Carranza by Obregón, and became, first, rector of the National University, and, in 1921, Minister of Education, until 1924. It was in this position that he accomplished his most remembered and important contributions, those which left a definite imprint in modern Mexico. The most visible of all are the murals that cover the walls of many public buildings and which gave Mexico a definite place in the world of art. The whole program was envisioned by Vasconcelos while traveling in Italy, and he turned the revolutionary government into the Maecenas of this public art for the masses. The result was a florescence of art unequaled in Mexican history, except in the barroque churches of the seventeenth century. But even more significant, and of farther reaching consequences than the muralist movement, was Vasconcelos' complete revamping of the whole system of education in Mexico, beginning with the creation of the Ministry of Education itself, which controlled public schools, art, libraries and museums. A program dedicated to the construction of public schools was carried out in every little village with unprecedented success and it still continues today. He was able to infuse his enthusiasm for public education into hundreds of young teachers who saw their mission to take education to the most remote villages as a continuation of the Revolution. Many sacrificed themselves to this noble cause, and the effects were felt not only in Mexico, but in other parts of Latin America, where public education programs on the pattern of the Mexican system were initiated and carried out with revolutionary fervor. His program of education stressed the technological skills as well as the humanities. Many folk arts and skills reflourished, while hundreds of classical books were printed in economical editions for mass consumption which Vasconcelos called "popular classics." His boast, "I got Latin America to read *The Iliad*," was certainly justified. Similar efforts were carried on for the protection and encouragement of music. He proved himself a stupendous administrator who put action ahead of theory. The Revolution would not have accomplished all it did without a man of his caliber.

But all this was not enough for Mexican politics, or perhaps he stepped on too many toes. In 1925, in opposition to the Calles administration, he resigned, and again exiled himself to Europe. Also this year, *La raza cósmica* was written and published in Spain. In 1926, he lectured at the University of Chicago and the University of Puerto Rico, and in 1928, published his *Metaphysics*. That same year, while lecturing at Stanford University, he received the news of Obregón's death, and speedily returned to Mexico to prepare himself to run as a presidential candidate in the coming election.[10] He was popular, but he lost the elections, and he went to Los Angeles to await further developments. However, although his followers and many impartial observers considered the elections fraudulent, no popular revolt arose to support his cause. Embittered, he continued his exile as an international intellectual and lecturer. Attempts at regaining political power failed repeatedly, and Vasconcelos did not return to Mexico until 1940. This political defeat has been considered traumatic by many of his biographers. One of his most dramatic acts was to formally rejoin the Catholic Church under the influence of Jesuit intellectuals. Yet, given his permanent though underlying bent towards religion and mysticism, this action was understandable. Equally understandable was his permanent defense of the Catholic-Spanish tradition, which for him meant Christianity, that is, the religion of Love or *Charitas*; a virtue which he strove to practice but often ignored. An always profound need for peace and withdrawal constantly battled within him against an equally profound need for political action, self-assertion and passion. Not many have braved such an internal turmoil and at the same time produced as much as did Vasconcelos. Part of him was a hermit, as he himself claimed, yet he was constantly pulled away from his retirement to become entangled in the web of Maya.

One of the most balanced descriptions of Vasconcelos' character was given by the Peruvian critic, Luis Alberto Sánchez, who knew him personally, although they were not close friends:

> The truth is that his was a contradictory personality: Ideologically, he moved from the Buddhist Nirvana to the absolute passion of a Torquemada; philosophically, from Pythagoras to Loyola; politically, from the leftist to the reactionary; socially, from Indianism to Hispanism, which among us means colonialism and plutocracy; in literature, from the essay to the novel.[11]

He was firm, however, in his antagonism towards the United States and the Anglo-Saxon world in general for the materialism and utilitarianism they represented.[12] He was often an extremist in his judgments of others, his ideals and his passions, but he died in peace in 1959.

III

Vasconcelos calls his philosophical system "Aesthetic Monism", indicating that the final essence of the universe is single (rather than double or plural) and that this essence is in a certain way "aesthetic."[13] This final essence, according to Vasconcelos, is energy, but as the light wave, which produces different colors according to its different rhythms, energy manifests itself in different forms according to its varying rhythms.

Three basic levels form the cosmological system, each corresponding to three basic types of rhythms; and to each corresponds a different mode of knowledge: The atomic level of mechanical movements (the field of science and logic); the level of living matter, characterized by directed, purposeful movement originating from within itself (its knowledge properly the field of ethics, according to Vasconcelos); and the level of the human psyche or soul, characterized by creativity, as in the aesthetic act, which encompasses any disinterested action (the field of aesthetics and mysticism).

However, of these three levels of rhythm (or "knowledge"), it is the aesthetic level that gives us the most accurate perception of the true essence of the universe, since in the aesthetic phenomena there is an identification or unification of rhythm between the object and the subject; the rhythms of the soul become attuned to the rhythms of the object, and vice versa. Thus the conclusion that the essence or basic rhythm of the universe is "aesthetic," that the essential nature of the cosmic energy manifests itself in the aesthetic phenomena.

The earliest expression of this line of thinking in Vasconcelos can be found in his first philosophical work, *Pitágoras: una teoría del ritmo*, in which the Pythagorean theory of numbers is interpreted by Vasconcelos as a symbolic representation of the rhythms the Pythagoreans perceived in the universe. When the rhythms of nature correspond to the inner rhythms of the soul, as in the aesthetic phenomenon, says Vasconcelos, a form of immediate perception takes place that is different from the intellectual or the sensorial. It was this affinity of rhythms, according to him, that the Pythagoreans expressed symbolically in their theory of numbers. Thus, the inner self is conceived as a rhythm which finds echo in the rhythms of nature. As a correlative to this metaphysics, Vasconcelos formulated a theory of knowledge which, although it does not reject logic and science, considers them limited tools for the knowledge of the essential nature of the universe:

> For that reason, the mystery of everything created is not solved by intelligence, nor by experience, whose ordered whole constitutes science, but only by the intuition of beauty. Only in art can the genders, classes, numbers, ideas, and beings be contemplated and fused together. Thus it has been understood by the mystics, because mysticism is essentially an aesthetics, a law of eternal beauty. In the melody, in the form, the mystic sense looks for the melodious permanence of the universe. The same laws rule art and mysticism, except that the artist sees from the outside, and the mystic from the inside. (*O.C.*, III, 50-51.)

The metaphysical basis for this theory of knowledge is the basic unity of the knower and the known:

> Going beyond rational functions and faculties, beyond reason itself, we say that the primitive, profound, synthetic sense of our conscience in its pure, total, energetic function, shows us that the phenomenon and the noumenon are born of the same fount, *which is inside ourselves* and appears either single or double; single when it simply is, and double when it contemplates and judges... (*O.C.*, III, 51-52, underlined in original text.)

According to Vasconcelos, the subject, or the knower, approaches the object in two ways. One, "in order to make use of it in some way, as Bergson says, for the purpose of action, thus creating the intellect, or properly speaking, the world of concrete facts and abstract ideas." (*O.C.*, III, 63.) In another way, the subject responds to the object in an independent and disinterested manner, as it occurs in the aesthetic experience or perception:

> . . . which does not lead to any concrete activity, but makes us participate in a new manner of existence, without the effort of purposefulness, yet animated with all the vigor of the most

intense life. Something similar to what happens with the parallel strings of a musical instrument. If a bow vibrates one of them, the rest, even without being touched by the bow, will vibrate with an undulation that is sympathetic to the string that was played. So the spirit, left to itself in the world, perceives the internal rhythms that regulate the objects and reaches a sympathetic vibration that attunes it to the universe. It would be a bad usage of terms to say that this is a new mode of knowledge, because this is not knowledge, but a new manner of existence, more real than the two which until today have been discussed by philosophy: The real and the ideal. This new mode of perception separates itself from both hypotheses of the real and the ideal, and it goes, so to speak, as if in-between the objects through the interstices left open by the conventional fixity of ideas, pursuing a reality whose mysterious flow is the true river of life, while the objects, and ideas, and everything else that operates on both of these is like the foam sprayed by the water of the river when it hits against the pebbles and rocks that divert its course. (*O.C.* III, 63-64)

This manner of attuning the inner self with the world, independent of sensitivity and ideas is what Vasconcelos calls the "sense of rhythm, an occult and marvelous sense that, undoubtedly, gives us the most profound impression of the world" (*O.C.*, III, 64). This sense of rhythm is manifested in the aesthetic emotion, thus, the aesthetic manner of perceiving the world or living in it is the ethical manifestation of such "knowledge".

This is not to say that the aesthetic emotion is the ultimate form of perception or of grasping the final essence of the universe. In one of his last books, *Todología*, Vasconcelos proposes a fourth level of rhythm beyond the manifest universe, which is the level of the Divine Person, the level of complete union attained in the mystical experience. In Vasconcelos, the relationship of the aesthetic to the divine is perhaps similar to that expressed by Aldous Huxley in his essay, "Some Reflections on Time": "Aesthetic goods are precious because they are symbolic of and analogous to the unitive knowledge of timeless reality."[14]

This early version of Vasconcelos' aesthetic theory in the *Pythagoras* was not basically changed in the more elaborate and mature philosophical writings of the *Metaphysics*, the *Ethics*, and the *Aesthetics*. (A fourth volume on Mysticism, to culminate this series, was never completed.) In the Prologue to *Todología: Filosofía de la coordinación* (México, 1956), Vasconcelos himself traces the development of his thought: "Chronologically, and also as a natural sequence, this is the final volume of a series that begins with my *Pythagoras* (1916), is continued in the *Metaphysics* (1929) and the *Ethics* (1931), acquires configuration in the *Aesthetics* (1935) and discovers its own methodology in the *Organic Logic* (1945)" (p. 6). There, he summarizes his system as: "A vision of the universe that begins with the magnetic wave and ends in the Trinity as defined by Saint Paul; this is what the present book tries to capture" (p. 9).

All these books center around the concept of aesthetic perception as rhythm; aesthetic perception being a state of unity or synchronization of the inner rhythms of the soul and the external rhythms of nature. A very concise but complete definition of Vasconcelos' system is given by Luis Washington Vita:

> This system is already outlined in his interpretation of the Pythagorean theory of numbers as a rhythmic theory, where the aesthetic-metaphysical characteristics predominate over the purely numerical and mathematical. But it was developed into a later system, thanks to the influence of Plotinus, which was repeatedly acknowledged by the author. Yet, Vasconcelos' aesthetic monism is not simply a revival of Plotinus' monistic emanationism because, on the one hand, Vasconcelos introduces in his concepts a modern notion of energy, which in his system, plays the same role as that which the idea of substance played in the ancient concepts of emanation. On the other hand, Vasconcelos conceives the evolution of the universe in an emergent sense, moving towards the transformation of cosmic energy into beauty, which is the supreme and the most perfect state of the primitive energy. Nevertheless, this is not to say that the Mexican thinker adopts an impersonal monism, but on the contrary, he accents more and more the strong motives of a personal character which underlie his philosophy, motives which, according to him, coincide with fundamental Christian and, especially, Catholic ideas.[15]

Thus, keeping in mind Vasconcelos' doctrine of Aesthetic Monism and his interpretation of the aesthetic mode of perceiving or living in the world, perhaps it may become clearer what Vasconcelos means by his description of the manner of life predicted for the Aesthetic Era and the prevalence of the Cosmic race. It is clear, for instance, the close relationship of Vasconcelos' description of the aesthetic mode with the state of bliss described in all mystic traditions. So that what Vasconcelos predicts for the future of mankind (somewhat like Teilhard de Chardin) is akin to a universal state of mystical union. The mixture of the races is but one aspect in which this tendency to an integration of rhythms guided by the aesthetic experience is manifested: "The instinct of sympathy pulsates at the bottom of all human relationships attracting or repelling according to that mystery we call taste, mystery which is the secret reason of all aesthetic" (p. 64 This ed.). It also becomes clear that the three stages in the development of humanity proposed by Vasconcelos in *La raza cósmica* correspond, to a certain extent, with the stages of the mystical process: 1) Liberation from the material, from the needs of the senses. 2) Liberation from the intellect and the illusions of the mind in general. 3) State of mystical union of which joy and love are essential manifestations.

Vasconcelos' essay on the Cosmic race, then, is not simply a racist theory, but a theory of the future development of human consciousness. It is impossible to interpret this essay correctly without taking into account the philosophical thought which Vasconcelos takes not only from modern Europe, from Bergson and Maine de Biran, but also from antiquity, from Plotinus and the School of Alexandria, from the mystic tradition, from Indian philosophy, and from the whole esoteric tradition, including twentieth century Theosophists, from whose writings, perhaps, the concept of the Cosmic race originates.[16] This concept, as well as the idea of the future Mystical Era of mankind, had already appeared in some of these writings, and was in vogue in the European climate of the turn of the century. It may have led to the Germanic concept of the Aryan race as a sort of Cosmic race, which culminated in the tragedy of Nazism. Vasconcelos escapes such narrow racism by proclaiming the disappearance of all known races, be they considered superior or inferior, and their fusion into one. In calling this possibility to the attention of the Hispanic world, Vasconcelos also offered them a possibility of redemption by continuing on their basic trend of universalism and unity, rather than by following

xxix

the dissociative tendencies of the materialistic cultures. Although Vasconcelos directed his essay to the Hispanic world, his ideas are, of course, of universal import, and the announcement of the new age continues to manifest itself in various ways, each day with greater urgency.

Notes

[1] Originally published in 1939, and later included as Chapter XIV in the book *The Vision of the Past* (New York: Harper, 1957, from the original French edition of the same year.)

[2] *Time*, (Oct. 16, 1964), 84:91-21.

[3] Tr. from *Ariel*, Ed. by G. Brotherson, (Cambridge Univ. Press, 1967), pp. 92-93.

[4] For a discussion of the concept of the Cosmic race in relation to Chicano identity, see: Leo Grebler, Joan W. Moore, and Ralph C. Guzmán, *The Mexican-American People: The Nation's Second Largest Minority* (New York: The Free Press, 1970). Also, Anthony Gary Dworkin, "The People of La Raza: The Mexican-Americans of Los Angeles" in Noel Pitts Gist and A.G. Dworkin, *The Blending of the Races: Marginality and Identity in World Perspective* (New York: Wiley-Interscience, 1972), Chap. 9, pp. 176-190.

[5] All quotes of Vasconcelos are my translations from his *Obras completas* (México: Limusa, 1957). Indicated as *O.C.* in the text.

[6] *Vasconcelos and His World* (New York: Las Americas, 1966), p. 292.

[7] Tr. from Antonio Sacoto, "Aspectos indigenistas de la obra literaria de José Vasconcelos (1881-1959)" *Cuadernos Americanos*, 163:151-157. See also *El indio en el ensayo de la América Española* (New York: Las Américas, 1971), pp. 115-123 by the same author.

[8] See Ronald Hilton's excellent short biography of "José Vasconcelos," *The Americas*, VII, pp. 395-412.

[9] See Daniel de Guzmán, *Carlos Fuentes* (New York: Twayne Publishers, 1972), pp. 21 and 154. On Madero, see: Francisco I. Madero: "Mis memorias," in *Pro-Madero* (México: Agrupación Pro-Madero, 1920?), pp. 131-150. Martín Luis Guzmán in *El águila y la serpiente* also recalls this aspect of Vasconcelos life around the year 1914: "José Vasconcelos empapaba ya su espíritu en las concepciones neoplatónicas y budistas del Universo y tenía jurada guerra sin cuartel — aunque no sin debilidades — a la mala bestia en cuyo cuerpo nuestras pobres almas sufren el castigo de encarnarse para vivir. Era, sin embargo, demasiado generoso para detenerse en una mera aspiración interior, así fuese honda. Y como riqueza y generosidad producen incongruencia, vivía con tanto ardor el torbellino de lo aparentemente sensible, como ponía fe en su doctrina, purificadora y liberadora." *Obras completas* (México: Compañía General de Ediciones, 1971) p. 324.

[10] For a well documented account of these crucial years in Vasconcelos' life see John Skirius, *José Vasconcelos y la cruzada de 1929* (México: Siglo XXI) 1978 and "Vasconcelos and México de Afuera (1928)" in *Aztlán. International Journal of Chicano Research*, vol. 7, núm. 3 (Fall 1976) pp. 479-496.

[11] Tr. from "El Vasconcelos que conozco," *Nueva Democracia*, New York, vol. 40, no. 4, 1960, p. 46.

[12] At least in public, in private he may have had other opinions. See John Skirius, *José Vasconcelos y la cruzada de 1929*, pp. 16 and 48.

[13] For a concise and fairly clear exposition of Vasconcelos' philosophical system, see Patrick Romanell, "Il monismo estetico di José Vasconcelos," *Rivista di Filosofia moderna*, Vol. 44, 1953, pp. 137-157. Romanell summarizes Vasconcelos' system in the following three principles: "Il monismo estetico in quanto sistema filosofico si basa su tre postulati relativi alla belleza che si implicano vicendevolmente é che hanno tutti una dichiarata origine mistica. I tre postulati sono:

1) La belleza é una particolare forma di energia cosmica.
2) La vera via per comprendere la natura della cose é l'emzione estetica.
3) L'universo non ha soltanto un moto di decadenza ma anche di progresso, diventando sempre piú bello."

For another concise and clear exposition of Vasconcelos' system, in English, see John H. Haddox, "The Aesthetic Philosophy of José Vasconcelos," *International Philosophical Quarterly*, Vol. 4, 1964, pp. 283-296.
For more extensive works, see bibliography in this edition.

[14] *Vedanta for Modern Man*, Ed. Christopher Isherwood, (New America Library: New York, 1972), p. 138.

[15] Este sistema já se entremostra em sua interpretaçao da teoría pitagórica como teoría rítmica, onde as categorias estético-metafísicas predominam sobre as puramente numéricas e matemáticas. Mas foi desenvolvida numa construçao posterior graças á influencia de Plotino, repetidamente reconhecida pelo autor. O monismo estético de Vasconcelos nao é poren, sómente uma revivifiçao do emanatismo monista plotiniano já que, por um lado, introduz éle em seus conceitos a noçao moderna de energía, que desempenha no sistema de Vasconcelos um papel análogo ao desempenhado nas antigas concepçoes emanatistas pelo idéia de substancia, e, por outro lado, concebe a evoluçao do universo num sentido emergentista, encaminhado para a transformaçao da energía cosmica em beleza, a qual é o estádio supremo e mais perfeito da energia primitiva. Contudo, nao quer isto dizer que o pensador mexicano adote um impersonalismo monista; pelo contrário, acentuou cada vez mais os fortes motivos da índole personalista que subjaziam en sua filosofia, motivos que, a seu ver, sao coincidentes com as idéais fundamentais cristás e, especialmente, católicas.

Luis Washington Vita, "José Vasconcelos (1882-1959)", *Revista mexicana de filosofía*, II, 3, 1959, p. 73.

[16] Another inspiration for the concept of the Cosmic race may have been Richard Maurice Bucke, *Cosmic Consciousness* (first published in 1901) which offers a vision of the future development of the human race in the light of evolutionary concepts and on the basis of, according to his data, an increasing frequency in the occurrence of mystical experiences, or "cosmic consciousness." This led him to postulate the evolutionary development of the human race towards a species gifted with cosmic consciousness, that is, with an expanded mode of consciousness beyond

the present day limitations of self consciousness, to a "higher form of consciousness than that possessed by the ordinary man" (Dutton: New York, 1969), p. 1.

Notes on the Present Edition

The first edition of *La raza cósmica. Misión de la raza iberoamericana. Notas de viaje a la América del Sur* was published in Spain in 1925, according to Vasconcelos. Copies of this edition that I have seen were printed in Barcelona for Agencia Mundial de Librería with no date. It consists of a "Prólogo" subtitled "Origen y objeto del continente — Latinos y sajones — Probable misión de ambas Américas — La quinta raza o la raza cósmica," and a section titled "Notas de Viaje" with sections on Brazil, Uruguay, and Argentina.

The second edition was published in Mexico: Espasa-Calpe Mexicana, and concurrently in Buenos Aires: Espasa-Calpe Argentina, in 1948. It incorporates a new "Prólogo" (the old prologue was now titled "El mestizaje") and a few corrections by the pen of Vasconcelos himself. Subsequent editions are based on this one.

In 1958, *La raza cósmica* was included in volume II of Vasconcelos' *Obras completas*, and in 1967, a new edition was published in Madrid by Aguilar.

The present edition is based on the text of the 1948 edition collated with the text of the first edition. It includes only the "Prólogo" of the 1948 edition and the main essay, "El mestizaje," leaving out the travel notes.

This bilingual annotated edition was prepared in response to a friend, Alfredo Beza, of San Antonio, Texas, who needed the English text for his students. Thus the explanatory notes are intended to provide general background to readers not quite familiar with Latin American history and culture, as well as to clarify certain points not familiar to the present day reader.

THE COSMIC RACE
The Mission of the Ibero American Race

Prologue to the 1948 Edition

The central thesis of this book is that the various races of the earth tend to intermix at a gradually increasing pace, and eventually will give rise to a new human type, composed of selections from each of the races already in existence. This prediction was first published[1] at a time when the Darwinist doctrine of natural selection, which preserves the fittest and dooms the weak, was still prevalent in the scientific world; a doctrine which, applied to the sociological field by Gobineau,[2] gave origin to the pure Aryan theory, supported by the English and carried to aberrant imposition by Nazism.

Opposition to this theory was voiced in France by biologists such as Leclerc du Sablon[3] and Noüy,[4] who interpreted evolution in a different way from Darwinism, even contrary to it. Furthermore, the sociological events of the last few years, in particular, the futility of the last great war,[5] which left everybody disgusted, when not ruined, have given rise to a current of more humane doctrines. Even distinguished Darwinists, old supporters of Spencerianism,[6] who disdained the dark and mestizo races, are now members of international organizations, such as UNESCO, which proclaim the need to abolish all racial discrimination and to educate all men in equality; nothing but the old Catholic doctrine that declared the Indian's fitness for the Holy Sacraments and, therefore, his right to marry a white or yellow consort.

Thus the predominant political doctrines acknowledge again the legality of mixed races and, with this, set the basis for an interracial fusion recognized by Law. If, to this, we add the fact that modern means of communication tend to suppress geographical barriers, and that generalized education will contribute to raise the economic standard of all men, it will be clear that all obstacles to an accelerated fusion of the races will gradually disappear.

In short, present world conditions favor the development of interracial sexual unions, a fact which lends unexpected support to the thesis which, for lack of a better name, I entitled: The future Cosmic Race.

Nevertheless, it remains to be seen whether the unlimited and inevitable mixture is a favorable factor to the increment of culture or if, to the

3

contrary, it will produce a decadence which now would no longer be of merely national but of worldwide proportions. This problem raises again the question the mestizo has often asked himself: Is my contribution to culture comparable to that of the relatively pure races that have made history up to our days, such as the Greeks, the Romans, or the Europeans? And, within each country, how do the periods of miscegenation compare with the periods of homogeneous racial creativity? So as not to overextend ourselves, we shall limit our observations to a few examples.

Beginning with the most ancient race in history, the Egyptian, recent observations have demonstrated that Egyptian civilization advanced from the south to the north, from the Upper Nile to the Mediterranean. A predominantly white and relatively homogeneous race created a flourishing First Great Empire around Luxor[7]. Wars and conquests weakened this empire and placed it at the mercy of black penetration, but the advance to the north was not interrupted. However, during a period of several centuries, the decadence of the culture was evident. It is presumable, then, that already by the time of the Second Empire, a new, mestizo race, with mixed characteristics of both the white and the black, had been produced. This is the race that brought about the Second Empire, more advanced and flourishing than the First. The period in which the pyramids were built, and the Egyptian civilization reached its summit, is a mestizo period.[8]

Greek historians are in agreement today that the Golden Age of Hellenic culture appeared as the result of a mixture of races. Here, however, the contrast between black and white was not present; it was rather a mixture of light colored races. Nonetheless, there was a mixture of races and cultural currents.

Greek civilization declines when the empire expands with Alexander, which facilitates the Roman conquest. Among Julius Caesar's troops, the new Roman mixture is already noticeable: Gallics, Spaniards, Britons, and even Germans, who collaborate in the feats of the Empire and transform Rome into a cosmopolitan center. It is a well-known fact that there were emperors of Hispanic-Roman blood.[9] At any rate, the contrasts were not too violent, since the mixture was essentially of European races. The invasions by Barbarians who mix with native Gallics, Spaniards, Celts, or Tuscans, produced the European nationalities that have been the fountainhead of modern culture.

Passing on to the New World, we see that the powerful North American nation has been nothing but a melting pot of European races. The

Blacks have actually remained apart in regards to the creation of power, yet the spiritual penetration they have accomplished through music, dance, and quite a few aspects of artistic sensitivity has had great importance.

After the United States, the nation with the most vigorous drive is the Argentine Republic, where the mixture of similar races, all of them of European origin, is again repeated. Here, Mediterranean types predominate, in contrast to the United States, where the Nordic types are predominant.

Thus, it can be readily stated that the mixture of similar races is productive, while the mixture of very distant types, as in the case of Spaniards and American Indians, has questionable results. The underdevelopment of the Hispanic American peoples, where the native element predominates, is difficult to explain, unless we go far back in time to the first example cited here of the Egyptian civilization. It so happens that the mixture of quite dissimilar elements takes a long time to mold. Among us, due to the exclusion of Spaniards decreed after Independence, the mixing of the races was interrupted before the racial type was completely finished. In countries like Ecuador or Peru, political motives, as well as the poverty of the land, restrained Spanish immigration.

At any rate, the most optimistic conclusion that can be drawn from the facts here observed is that even the most contradictory racial mixtures can have beneficial results, as long as the spiritual factor contributes to raise them. In fact, the decline of Asiatic peoples can be attributed to their isolation, but also, and without doubt, primarily, to the fact that they have not been Christianized.[10] A religion such as Christianity made the American Indians advance, in a few centuries, from cannibalism to a relative degree of civilization.

5

Mestizaje

I

In the opinion of respectable geologists, the American continent includes some of the most ancient regions of the world. The Andes are, undoubtedly, as old as any other mountain range on earth. And while the land itself is ancient, the traces of life and human culture also go back in time beyond any calculations. The architectural ruins of legendary Mayans, Quechuas, and Toltecs are testimony of civilized life previous to the oldest foundations of towns in the Orient and Europe.[11] As research advances, more support is found for the hypothesis of Atlantis as the cradle of a civilization that flourished millions of years ago in the vanished continent and in parts of what is today America.[12] The thought of Atlantis evokes the memory of her mysterious predecessors. The Hiperborean continent, vanished without trace, other than the vestiges of life and culture sometimes discovered under the snows of Greenland; the Lemurians or the black race from the south; the Atlantean civilization of the red men; immediately afterwards, the emergence of the yellow races, and finally the civilization of the white men.[13] This profound legendary[14] hypothesis explains the evolution of the races better than the elucubrations of geologists like Ameghino,[15] who places the origin of man in Patagonia, a land which, it is well known, is of recent geological formation. On the other hand, the hypothesis of prehistoric ethnic empires finds extraordinary support in Wegener's theory of the translation of continents.[16] According to this thesis, all the lands were previously united into a single continent, which has since been breaking apart. Thus, it is easy to assume that in a particular region of a continuous land mass, a race would develop which, after progress and decline, would be substituted by another, instead of having recourse to the hypothesis of migrations from one continent to another by means of disappearing land bridges. It is also interesting to note another coincidence of the ancient tradition with the most recent facts from geology: According to Wegener, the communication between Australia, India, and Madagascar was interrupted before the communication between South America and Africa. This amounts to a corroboration of the theory that the site of the Lemurian civilization disappeared before the flourishing of Atlantis, and also, that the last continent to disappear was Atlantis, since scientific explorations have come to demonstrate that the Atlantic Ocean is the sea of most recent formation.

Although the origins of this theory remain more or less confused within a tradition as obscure as it is rich in meaning, the legend still remains of a civilization born in our forests, or spread to them after a powerful growth. Traces of it are still visible in Chichén Itzá and Palenque,[17] and in all the sites where the Atlantean mystery prevails: The mystery of the red men who, after dominating the world, had the precepts of their wisdom engraved on the Emerald Table,[18] perhaps a marvelous Colombian emerald, which at the time of the telluric upheavals was taken to Egypt, where Hermes[19] and his adepts learned and transmitted its secrets.

If we are, then, geologically ancient, as well as in respect to the tradition, how can we still continue to accept the fiction, invented by our European fathers, of the novelty of a continent that existed before the appearance of the land from where the discoverers and conquerors came?

The question has paramount importance to those who insist in looking for a plan in History. The confirmation of the great antiquity of our continent may seem idle to those who see nothing in the chain of events but a fateful repetition of meaningless patterns. With boredom we should regard the work of contemporary civilization, if the Toltec palaces would tell us nothing else but that civilizations pass away leaving no other fruit than a few carved stones piled upon each other or forming arched vaults or roofs of two planes intersecting at an angle. Why begin again, if within four or five thousand years other new immigrants will distract their leisure by pondering upon the remains of our trivial contemporary architecture? Scientific history becomes confused and leaves unanswered all these ruminations. Empirical history, suffering from myopia, loses itself in details, but it cannot determine a single antecedent for historical times. It flees from general conclusions, from transcendental hypotheses, to fall into the puerility of the description of utensils and cranial indices and so many other, merely external, minutiae that lack importance when seen apart from a vast and comprehensive theory.

Only a leap of the spirit, nourished with facts, can give us a vision that will lift us above the micro-ideology of the specialist. Then we can dive deeply into the mass of events in order to discover a direction, a rhythm, and a purpose. Precisely there, where the analyst discovers nothing, the synthesizer and the creator are enlightened. Let us, then, attempt explanations, not with the fantasy of the novelist, but with an intuition supported by the facts of history and science.

The race that we have agreed to call Atlantean prospered and declined in America. After its extraordinary flourishment, after having completed its cycle and fulfilled its particular mission, it entered the silence and went into decline until being reduced to the lesser Aztec and Inca empires, totally unworthy of the ancient and superior culture. With the decline of the Atlanteans, the intense civilization was transported to other sites and changed races: It dazzled in Egypt; it expanded in India and Greece, grafted onto new races. The Aryans mixed with the Dravidians[20] to produce the Hindustani, and at the same time, by means of other mixtures, created Hellenic culture.

Greece laid the foundations of Western or European civilization; the white civilization that, upon expanding, reached the forgotten shores of the American continent in order to consummate the task of re-civilization and re-population. Thus we have the four stages and the four racial trunks: the Black, the Indian, the Mongol, and the White. The latter, after organizing itself in Europe, has become the invader of the world, and has considered itself destined to rule, as did each of the previous races during their time of power. It is clear that domination by the whites will also be temporary, but their mission is to serve as a bridge. The white race has brought the world to a state in which all human types and cultures will be able to fuse with each other. The civilization developed and organized in our times by the whites has set the moral and material basis for the union of all men into a fifth universal race, the fruit of all the previous ones and amelioration of everything past.

White culture is migratory, yet it was not Europe as a whole that was in charge of initiating the reintegration of the red world into the modality of preuniversal culture, which had been represented for many centuries by the white man. The transcendental mission fell upon the two most daring branches of the European family, the strongest and most different human types: the Spanish and the English.

***

From the start, from the time of the discovery and the conquest, it was the Castilians and the British (or the Latins and the Anglo-Saxons, if we include the Portuguese, on one side, and the Dutch, on the other) the ones who accomplished the task of beginning a new period of history by conquering and populating the new hemisphere. Although they may have thought of themselves simply as colonizers, as carriers of culture, in reality, they were establishing the basis for a period of general and definitive transformation. The so-called Latins, well endowed with genius and courage, seized the best regions, the ones they thought were the richest, while the English had to be satisfied with what was left to them by a more capable people. Neither Spain nor Portugal allowed the Anglo-Saxons to come near their domains, and I do not mean for reasons of war, but not even to take part in commerce. Latin predominance was unquestionable at the beginning. No one would have suspected at the time of the Papal arbitration which divided the New World between Spain and Portugal[21] that, a few centuries later, the New World would no longer be Spanish nor Portuguese but English. No one would have imagined that the humble colonists of the Hudson and the Delaware, so peaceful and diligent, would go on taking over, step by step, the best and largest expansions of land, until they formed a republic which today constitutes one of the largest empires in History.

Our age became, and continues to be, a conflict of Latinism against Anglo-Saxonism; a conflict of institutions, aims and ideals. It marks the climax of a secular fight that begins with the disaster of the Invincible Armada and gets worse with the defeat of Trafalgar.[22] Since then, the location of the conflict began to change and was transferred to the new continent, where it still had fateful episodes. The defeats of Santiago de Cuba, Cavite, and Manila[23] were distant but logical echoes of the catastrophes of the Invincible and Trafalgar. Now the conflict is set entirely in the New World. In History, centuries tend to be like days; thus it is not strange at all that we still cannot completely discard the impression of defeat. We are going through times of despair, we continue to lose not only geographic sovereignty, but moral power. Far from feeling united in the face of disaster, our determination is dispersed in search of small and vain goals. Defeat has brought us the confusion of values and concepts; the victor's diplomacy deceives us after defeating us; commerce conquers us with its small advantages. Despoiled of our previous greatness, we boast of an exclusively national patriotism and we do not even see the dangers that threaten our race as a whole. We deny ourselves to each other. Defeat has debased us to the point that, without even being aware of it, we serve the ends of the enemy policy of defeating us one by one; of offering particular advantages to some of our brothers while the vital interests of the others are sacrificed. Not only were we defeated in combat; ideologically, the Anglos continue to conquer us. The greatest battle was lost on the day that each one of the Iberian republics went forth alone, to live her own life apart from her sisters, concerting treaties and receiving false benefits, without tending to the common interests of the race. The founders of our new nationalism were, without knowing it, the best allies of the Anglo-Saxons, our rivals in the possession of the continent. The unfurling of our twenty banners at the Pan American Union[24] in Washington, should be seen as a joke played by skillful enemies. Yet, each of us takes pride in our humble rags, expression of a vain illusion, and we do not even blush at the fact of our discord in the face of the powerful North American union. We ignore the contrast presented by Anglo-Saxon unity in opposition to the anarchy and solitude of the Ibero American emblems. We keep ourselves jealously independent from each other, yet one way or another we submit to, or ally ourselves with, the Anglo-Saxon union. Not even the national unity of the five Central American states has been possible, because a stranger has not granted us his approval and because we lack the true patriotism to sacrifice the present for the future. A lack of creative thinking and an excess of critical zeal, which we have certainly borrowed from other cultures, takes us to fruitless discussions in which our common aspirations are denied as often as they are ascertained. Yet, we do not realize that, in times of action, and despite all the doubts of English thinkers, the English seek the alliance of their American or Australian brothers, and the Yankee feels as English as the Englishman from England. We shall not be great as long as the Spaniard from America does not feel as much a Spaniard as the sons of Spain. This does not preclude that we may differ whenever necessary, as long as we do not drift away from the higher common mission. This is the way we have to act, if we are to allow the Iberian culture to finish producing all its fruits; if we are going to keep Anglo-Saxon culture from remaining triumphant in America without opposition. It is futile to imagine other solutions. Civilization is neither improvised nor curtailed, nor can it grow out of the paper of a political constitution. It always derives from a long, secular preparation and purification of elements that are transmitted and combined from the beginning of History. For that reason, it is stupid to initiate our patriotism with Father Hidalgo's cry of independence,[25] or the conspiration of Quito,[26] or the feats of Bolívar,[27] because if we do not root it in Cuauhtemoc[28] and Atahualpa,[29] it will have no support. At the same time, it is necessary to trace our patriotism back to our Hispanic fountainhead and educate it on the lessons we should derive from the defeats, which are also ours, of Trafalgar and the Invincible Armada. If our patriotism is not identified with the different stages of the old conflict between Latins and Anglo-Saxons, it shall never overcome a regionalism lacking in universal breadth. We shall fatefully see it degenerate into the narrowness and myopia of parochialism, or into the impotent inertia of a mollusk attached to its rock.

So that we shall not be forced to deny our own fatherland, it is necessary that we live according to the highest interests of the race, even though this may not be yet in the highest interest of humanity. It is true that the heart is not satisfied with less than a full-fledged internationalism, but given the present world conditions, internationalism would only serve to consummate the triumph of the strongest nations; it would only serve the aims of the English. Even the Russians, with their two hundred million population, have had to postpone their theoretical inter-nationalism, in order to devote themselves to the support of oppressed nationalities such as India and Egypt. At the same time, they have strengthened their own nationalism in order to defend themselves against a disintegration which could only favor the great imperialist states. It would, then, be puerile for weak countries like ours, to start denying what is rightfully theirs in the name of aims that could not crystalize in reality. The present state of civilization still imposes patriotism on us as a necessity for the defense of material and moral interests; but it is indis-pensable for this patriotism to seek vast and transcendental aims. Its mission was cut short, in a sense, with independence. Now it is necessary to bring it back to the flow of its universal historical destiny.

The first stage of the profound conflict was decided in Europe and we lost. Afterwards, when all the advantages were on our side in the New World, since Spain had conquered America, the Napoleonic stupidity gave Louisiana away to the Englishmen from this side of the ocean, to the Yankees; this decided the fate of the New World in favor of the Anglo-Saxons. The "genius of war" could see no farther than the miserable boundary disputes between puny European states, and did not realize that the cause of Latinism, which he claimed to represent, was defeated on the same day that the Empire was proclaimed, by the sole fact that the common destiny was placed in the hands of an incompetent. On the other hand, European prejudice hid the fact that, in America, the conflict that Napoleon could not comprehend in its full transcendence had already

12

acquired universal dimensions. Napoleon, in his foolishness, was not able to surmise that the destiny of the European races was going to be decided in the New World. When, in the most thoughtless manner, he destroyed French power in America, he also weakened the Spaniards. He betrayed us and placed us at the mercy of the common enemy. Without Napoleon, the United States would not exist as a world empire, and Louisiana, still French, would have to be part of the Latin American Confederation. The defeat of Trafalgar, then, would have been irrelevant. None of these facts were even considered because the destiny of the race was in the hands of a fool, because caesarism is the scourge of the Latin race.

Napoleon's betrayal of the global destiny of France mortally wounded the Spanish empire in America at the moment of its greatest weakness. The English-speaking people took possession of Louisiana without combat, reserving their ammunitions for the now easy conquest of Texas and California. Without the base of the Mississippi, the English, who call themselves Yankees out of a simple richness of expression, would not have been able to take possession of the Pacific; they would not be the masters of the continent today; they would have remained in a sort of Netherlands transplanted to America, and the New World would be Spanish and French. Bonaparte made it Anglo-Saxon.

It is clear, of course, that not merely the external causes, the treaties, wars, and policies, determine the destinies of nations. Figures like Napoleon are nothing but marks of vanity and corruption. The decadence of manners, the loss of public liberties, and the general ignorance have the effect of paralyzing the energy of a whole race at any given time.

The Spaniards went to the New World with the overflow of vigor left after the success of the Reconquest. Free men like Cortez,[30] Pizarro,[31] Alvarado,[32] and Belalcazar[33] were not caesars nor lackeys, but great captains that joined destructive impetus to creative genius. Immediately after victory, they traced the plans of the new cities and wrote the statutes of their foundation. Later, at the hour of bitter disputes with the metropolis, they knew how to return insult for insult, as did one of the Pizarros in a famous trial. They all felt equal before the king, like the Cid, like the great writers of the Golden Age felt, as all free men feel during epochs of greatness.

But as the conquest was being completed, the new organization began to fall into the hands of courtiers and favorites of the king: Incompetent men, not only for conquest, but even for the defense of what others had conquered with their talent and courage; degenerate courtiers, capable of oppressing and humiliating the natives, but submissive before the royal power. They and their masters did nothing else but spoil the work of Spanish genius in America. The portentous work started by iron-willed conquerors and consummated by wise and selfless missionaries was gradually annulled. A series of foreign monarchs, so justly painted by Velazquez[34] and Goya[35] in the company of dwarfs, buffoons, and courtiers, completed the disaster of colonial administration. The mania for imitating the Roman empire, which has caused so much harm in Spain, as well as in Italy and France, with its militarism and absolutism, brought about our decadence. At the same time our rivals, strengthened by virtue, grew and expanded in freedom.

Along with their growth in material strength, their practical ingenuity and intuition of success increased. The old colonists of New England and Virginia severed themselves from England only to grow better and become stronger. Political separation has never been an obstacle between England and her former colonies to maintain their unity and agreement in regards to the business of their common ethnic mission. Emancipation, instead of debilitating the great race, made it branch off, multiply, and spread, all-powerful, over the whole world, out of the impressive nucleus of one of the largest empires of all times. Since then, what is not conquered by the English of the Isles, is taken over and kept by the English of the new continent.

On the other hand, we Spaniards by blood or by culture, began by denying our traditions at the moment of our emancipation. We broke off with the past, and some even denied their blood saying it would have been better if the conquest of our regions had been accomplished by the English. Such words of treason may be excused only as actions brought about by tyranny and as the blindness engendered by defeat, but to lose the historical sense of a race in this way borders on the absurd. It is the same as denying our strong and wise parents when it is we, and not them, who are guilty of our decadence.

At any rate, the anti-Hispanic preaching and the corresponding anglicizing, skillfully spread by the English themselves, perverted our judgment from the beginning. It made us forget that we also have our share in the affront of Trafalgar. The meddling of English officers in the high ranks of our armies of independence would have ended by dishonoring us, were it not for the old pride of blood that came back to life in the

14

face of insult and punished the pirates of Albion[36] each time they approached with the intention of perpetrating a raid. Our ancestral rebelliousness knew how to reply with cannonades, in Buenos Aires as well as in Veracruz, Havana, Campeche and Panama,[37] every time the English corsair attacked. Disguised as pirates in order to avoid the responsibilities of defeat, the English were confident of attaining, if victorious, a place of honor among the British nobility.

Despite this firm unity against an invading enemy, our war of independence was limited by provincialism and by the absence of transcendental plans. The race that had dreamed of a world empire, that presumed to be descendents of the Roman glory, fell into the puerile satisfaction of creating little nations and sovereign principalities, encouraged by mentalities that saw a wall and not a summit in each mountain range. Our liberators, with the illustrious exceptions of Bolivar and Sucre,[38] the black Petion,[39] and no more than half a dozen others, were dreaming of Balkan glories. The rest, obsessed with the local outlook and entangled in a confused pseudo-revolutionary phraseology, simply busied themselves in belittling a conflict that could have been the beginning of the awakening of a whole continent. To divide, to tear to pieces the dream of a great Latin confederation, seemed to have been the goal of some of the ignorant practical men who fought for independence. Although they deserve their place of honor in this movement, they did not know how to follow, or did not even want to listen to the wise warnings of Bolivar.

It is clear that in every social development, the profound, inevitable causes that determine a given moment have to be taken into account. Our geography, for example, was and continues to be an obstacle to unity, but if we are to overcome this obstacle, first it will be necessary that we put order in our spirit by purifying our ideas and delineating precise orientations. As long as we are not able to correct our concepts, it will not be possible to influence the physical environment to make it serve our purposes.

In Mexico, for instance, except for Mina,[40] almost no one thought of the interests of the continent; worse yet, for a whole century the vernacular patriotism taught that we had triumphed over Spain thanks to the indomitable valor of our soldiers. At the same time, the *Cortes* of Cadiz and the uprisings against Napoleon,[41] which electrified the whole race, went almost without mention, as did the victories and sufferings of the sister nations of the continent. This error, common to all of our countries, is the result of times when history is written in order to please the despots.

15

Boastful patriotism is not satisfied with presenting its heroes as unities of a continental movement, but as autonomous, not realizing that in acting this way, it belittles rather than exalts them.

Such aberrations may also be explained because the indigenous element had not, and has not yet been fused in its totality with the Spanish blood. But this discord is more apparent than real: Should one talk to the most exalted Indianist of the convenience of adapting ourselves to Latinism, he will raise no questions; but tell him that our culture is Spanish and he will immediately bring up counter arguments. The stain from the spilled blood still remains. It is an accursed stain that centuries have not erased, but which the common danger must annul. There is no other recourse. Even the pure Indians are Hispanized, they are Latinized, just as the environment itself is Latinized. Say what one may, the red men, the illustrious Atlanteans from whom Indians derive, went to sleep millions of years ago, never to awaken. There is no going back in History, for it is all transformation and novelty. No race returns. Each one states its mission, accomplishes it, and passes away. This truth rules in Biblical times as well as in our times; all the ancient historians have formulated it. The days of the pure whites, the victors of today, are as numbered as were the days of their predecessors. Having fulfilled their destiny of mechanizing the world, they themselves have set, without knowing it, the basis for a new period: The period of the fusion and mixing of all peoples. The Indian has no other door to the future but the door of modern culture, nor any other road but the road already cleared by Latin civilization. The white man, as well, will have to depose his pride and look for progress and ulterior redemption in the souls of his brothers from other castes. He will have to diffuse and perfect himself in each of the superior varieties of the species, in each of the modalities that multiply revelation and make genius more powerful.

**

In the process of our ethnic mission, the war of emancipation from Spain signals a dangerous crisis. I do not mean that this war should not have been waged or should not have succeeded. In certain epochs, the transcendental end must be postponed: The race can wait while the fatherland presses upon us, and the fatherland is the immediate and indispensable present. It was impossible to continue depending on a sceptre which from mishap to mishap, and from misfortune to embarrassment had been going down until it fell into the dishonored hands of a Ferdinand VII.[42] The organization of a free Castilian Federation could have been worked out at the *Cortes* of Cadiz. The monarchy could not have been answered except by the defeat of its envoys. On this point, Mina's vision was complete: First, to establish freedom in the New World, and later, to overthrow the monarchy in Spain. Since the imbecility of the times kept this genial design from fulfillment, at least, let us try to keep it present in our minds. Let us recognize that it was a disgrace not to have proceeded with the cohesion demonstrated by those to the north, that prodigious race which we are accustomed to lavish with insults only because they have won each hand at the secular fight. They triumph because they join to their practical talents the clear vision of a great destiny. They keep present the intuition of a definite historical mission, while we get lost in the labyrinth of verbal chimeras. It seems as if God Himself guided the steps of the Anglo-Saxon cause, while we kill each other on account of dogma or declare ourselves atheists. How those mighty empire builders must laugh at our groundless arrogance and Latin vanity! They do not clutter their mind with the Ciceronian weight of phraseology, nor have they in their blood the contradictory instincts of a mixture of dissimilar races, *but they committed the sin of destroying those races, while we assimilated them, and this gives us new rights and hopes for a mission without precedent in History.*

For this reason, adverse obstacles do not move us to surrender, for we vaguely feel that they will help us to discover our way. Precisely in our differences, we find the way. If we simply imitate, we lose. If we discover and create, we shall overcome. The advantage of our tradition is that it has greater facility of sympathy towards strangers. This implies that our civilization, with all defects, may be the chosen one to assimilate and to transform mankind into a new type; that within our civilization, the warp, the multiple and rich plasma of future humanity is thus being prepared. This mandate from History is first noticed in that abundance of love that allowed the Spaniard to create a new race with the Indian and the Black, profusely spreading white ancestry through the soldier who begat a native family, and Occidental culture through the doctrine and example of the missionaries who placed the Indians in condition to enter into the new stage, the stage of world One. Spanish colonization created mixed races, this signals its character, fixes its responsibility, and defines its future. The English kept on mixing only with the whites and annihilated the natives. Even today, they continue to annihilate them in a sordid and economic fight, more efficient yet than armed conquest. This proves their limitation and is indication of their decadence. The situation is equivalent, in a larger scale, to the incestuous marriages of the pharaohs which undermined the virtues of the race; and it contradicts the ulterior goals of History to attain the fusion of peoples and cultures. To build an English world and to exterminate the red man, so that Northern Europe could be renovated all over an America made up with pure whites, is no more than a repetition of the triumphant process of a conquering race. This was already attempted by the red man and by all strong and homogeneous races, but it does not solve the human problem. America was not kept in reserve for five thousand years for such a petty goal. The purpose of the new and ancient continent is much more important. Its predestination obeys the design of constituting the cradle of a fifth race into which all nations will fuse with each other to replace the four races that have been forging History apart from each other. The dispersion will come to an end on American soil; unity will be consummated there by the triumph of fecund love and the improvement of all the human races. In this fashion, the synthetic race that shall gather all the treasures of History in order to give expression to universal desire shall be created.

The so-called Latin peoples, because they have been more faithful to their divine mission in America, are the ones called upon to consummate this mission. Such fidelity to the occult design is the guarantee of our triumph.

Even during the chaotic period of independence, which deserves so much censure, one can notice, however, glimpses of that eagerness for universality which already announced the desire to fuse humanity into a universal and synthetic type. Needless to say, Bolivar, partly because he realized the danger into which we were falling by dividing ourselves into isolated nationalities, and partly because of his gift for prophecy, formulated the plan for an Ibero-American Federation which some fools still question today.

It is true that, in general, the other leaders of Latin American independence did not have a clear conception of the future. Carried away by a provincialism that today we call patriotism, or by a limitation that today is dubbed national sovereignty, every one of them was only concerned with the immediate fate of their own people. Yet, it is also surprising to

18

observe that almost all of them felt animated by a humane and universal sentiment which coincides with the destiny that today we assign to the Latin American continent. Hidalgo, Morelos,[43] Bolivar, Petion the Haitian, the Argentinians in Tucuman,[44] Sucre, all were concerned with the liberation of the slaves, with the declaration of the equality of all men by natural right, and with the civil and social equality of Whites, Blacks and Indians. In a moment of historical crisis, they formulated the transcendental mission assigned to that region of the globe: The mission of fusing all peoples ethnically and spiritually.

Thus, what no one even thought of doing on the Anglo-Saxon area of the continent was done on the Latin side. In the north, the contrary thesis continued to prevail: The confessed or tacit intention of cleaning the earth of Indians, Mongolians or Blacks, for the greater glory and fortune of the Whites. In fact, since that time, the systems which, continuing to the present, have placed the two civilizations on opposing sociological fields were very well defined. The one wants exclusive dominion by the Whites, while the other is shaping a new race, a synthetic race that aspires to engulf and to express everything human in forms of constant improvement. If it were necessary to adduce proof, it would be sufficient to observe the increasing and spontaneous mixing which operates among all peoples in all of the Latin continent; in contrast with the inflexible line that separates the Blacks from the Whites in the United States, and the laws,each time more rigorous, for the exclusion of the Japanese and Chinese from California.[45]

The so-called Latins insist on not taking the ethnic factor too much into account for their sexual relations, perhaps because from the beginning they are not, properly speaking, Latins but a conglomeration of different types and races. Whatever opinions one may express in this respect, and whatever repugnance caused by prejudice one may harbor, the truth is that the mixture of races has taken place and continues to be consummated. It is in this fusion of ethnic stocks that we should look for the fundamental characteristic of Ibero-American idiosyncrasy. It may happen sometimes and, in fact, it has already happened, that economic competition may force us to close our doors, as is done by the Anglo-Saxons, to an unrestrained influx of Asians. But, in doing so, we obey reasons of economic order. We recognize that it is not fair that people like the Chinese, who, under the saintly guidance of Confucian morality multiply like mice, should come to degrade the human condition precisely at the moment when we begin to understand that intelligence serves to refrain and regulate the lower zoological instincts, which are contrary to a truly religious conception of life. If we reject the Chinese, it is because man, as he progresses, multiplies less, and feels the horror of numbers, for the same reason that he has begun to value quality. In the United States, Asians are rejected because of the same fear of physical overflow, characteristic of superior stocks; but also because Americans simply do not like Asians, even despise them, and would be incapable of intermarriage with them. The ladies of San Francisco have refused to dance with officials of the Japanese Navy, who are men as clean, intelligent, and, in their way, as handsome as those of any other navy in the world. Yet, these ladies will never understand that a Japanese may be handsome. Nor is it easy to convince the Anglo-Saxon that if the yellow and the black races have their characteristic smell, the Whites, for a foreigner, also have theirs, even though we may not be aware of it. In Latin America, the repulsion of one blood that confronts another strange blood also exists, but infinitely more attenuated. There, a thousand bridges are available for the sincere and cordial fusion of all races. The ethnic barricading of those to the north in contrast to the much more open sympathy of those to the south is the most important factor, and at the same time, the most favorable to us, if one reflects even superficially upon the future, because it will be seen immediately that we belong to tomorrow, while the Anglo-Saxons are gradually becoming more a part of yesterday. The Yankees will end up building the last great empire of a single race, the final empire of White supremacy. Meanwhile, we will continue to suffer the vast chaos of an ethnic stock in formation, contaminated by the fermentation of all types, but secure of the avatar into a better race. In Spanish America, Nature will no longer repeat one of her partial attempts. This time, the race that will come out of the forgotten Atlantis will no longer be a race of a single color or of particular features. The future race will not be a fifth, or a sixth race, destined to prevail over its ancestors. What is going to emerge out there is the definitive race, the synthetical race, the integral race, made up of the genius and the blood of all peoples and, for that reason, more capable of true brotherhood and of a truly universal vision.

In order to come near this sublime purpose, it is necessary to keep on creating, so to speak, the cellular tissue which will serve as the flesh and support of this new biological formation. In order to create that Protean, malleable, profound, ethereal, and essential tissue, it will be necessary for the Ibero-American race to permeate itself with its mission and embrace it as a mysticism.

Perhaps there is nothing useless in historical developments. Our own physical isolation and the mistake of creating nations, together with the original mixture of bloods, has served to keep us from the Anglo-Saxon limitation of constituting castes of pure races. History shows that these prolonged and rigorous selections produce types of physical refinement, interesting but lacking in vigor. They have a strange beauty, like that of the Brahmanic caste, but are decadent in the end. Never have they been seen to surpass other men, neither in talent, in goodness, or in strength. The road we have initiated is much more daring. It breaks away from ancient prejudices, and it would be almost unexplainable if it were not grounded on a sort of clamor that reaches from a remote distance, a distance which is not that of the past, but that mysterious distance from where the presage of the future comes.

If Latin America were just another Spain, to the same extent that the United States is another England, then the old conflict of the two stocks would do nothing else but to repeat its episodes on a vaster territory, and one of the two rivals would end up prevailing and imposing itself. But this is not the natural law of conflicts, neither in mechanics nor in life. Opposition and fight, particularly when transposed to the field of the spirit, serve to better define the contenders, to take each one to the summit of its destiny and, in the end, to join them into a common and victorious superiority.

The Anglo-Saxon mission has been accomplished sooner than ours because it was more immediate and was already known to History. In order to accomplish it, all that was necessary was to follow the example of other victorious people. Being mere continuators of Europe in the region of the continent they occupied, the values of the Whites reached the zenith. This is why the history of North America is like the uninterrupted and vigorous allegro of a triumphal march.

How different the sounds of the Ibero-American development! They resemble the profound scherzo of a deep and infinite symphony: Voices that bring accents from Atlantis; depths contained in the pupil of the red man, who knew so much, so many thousand years ago, and now seems to have forgotten everything. His soul resembles the old Mayan *cenote*[46] of green waters, laying deep and still, in the middle of the forest, for so many centuries since, that not even its legend remains any more. This

21

infinite quietude is stirred with the drop put in our blood by the Black, eager for sensual joy, intoxicated with dances and unbridled lust. There also appears the Mongol, with the mystery of his slanted eyes that see everything according to a strange angle, and discover I know not what folds and newer dimensions. The clear mind of the White, that resembles his skin and his dreams, also intervenes. Judaic striae hidden within the Castilian blood since the days of the cruel expulsion now reveal themselves, along with Arabian melancholy, as a remainder of the sickly Muslim sensuality. Who has not a little of all this, or does not wish to have all? There is the Hindu, who also will come, who has already arrived by way of the spirit, and although he is the last one to arrive, he seems the closest relative... So many races that have come and others that will come. In this manner, a sensitive and ample heart will be taking shape within us; a heart that embraces and contains everything and is moved with sympathy, but, full of vigor, imposes new laws upon the world. And we foresee something like another head that will dispose of all angles in order to fulfill the miracle of surpassing the sphere.

II

After examining the close and the remote possibilities of the mixed race that inhabits the Ibero-American continent, as well as the destiny that drives it to become the first synthetic race of the earth, it is necessary to inquire if the physical milieu within which this human stock is being developed corresponds to the ends determined by its bionomy. The territorial expanse already at its disposal is enormous. There is no land problem, then. The fact that its coasts do not have many first rate harbors is of almost no importance, given the ever increasing engineering advances. On the other hand, all the essential elements are, without doubt, abundant in quantities that surpass those of any other region on earth: Natural resources, arable land, water, and favorable climate. In regards to the latter factor, some will raise, of course, an objection: The climate, it will be said, is adverse to the new race, because the greatest part of the available land is located in the hottest region of the earth. However, this is precisely the advantage and the secret of the future. The great civilizations began in the Tropics and the final civilization will return to the Tropics. The new race will begin to fulfill its destiny as new means are invented to combat the heat insofar as it is adverse to man, yet leaving intact its benefic power for the production of life. The triumph of the Whites began with the conquest of snow and cold. The basis of white civilization is fuel. First, it served as a protection against the long winters. Then, it was discovered that its power could be used not only for warmth, but also for work; and the motor was born. And so it is that, from the hearth and the stove proceed all the machinery that is transforming the world. A similar invention would have been impossible in warm Egypt and, in fact, did not occur there, despite the fact that the Egyptians infinitely surpassed the intellectual capacity of the English race. To corroborate the last statement, it is sufficient to compare the sublime metaphysics of the *Book of the Dead*[47] of the Egyptian priests, with the vulgarity of Spencerian Darwinism. The chasm that separates Spencer from Hermes Trismegistus cannot be crossed by the blond dolichocephalics even in another thousand years of training and selection.

On the other hand, the English ship, that marvelous machine that proceeds from the Vikings of the north, was not even dreamed of by the Egyptians. The rude fight against the environment forced the Whites to devote their aptitudes to the conquest of temporal nature, and it is precisely this what constitutes their contribution to the civilization of the future. The Whites taught the control of matter. The science of the Whites will some day revert the method employed to attain control over fire and, instead, will make use of condensed snows, electrochemical currents, or subtle magic gases to destroy flies and pests and dissipate the sultry weather and the fevers. Then the whole world will spread over the Tropics and, in the solemn immensity of its landscapes, souls will conquer plenitude.

At the beginning, the Whites will try to take advantage of their inventions for their own benefit, but since science is no longer esoteric, it is not likely that they will succeed. They will be absorbed in the avalanche of all the other races, and, finally, deposing their pride, they will combine with the rest to make the new racial synthesis, the fifth race of the future.

The conquest of the Tropics will transform all aspects of life. Architecture will abandon the Gothic arch, the vault, and, in general, the roof, which answers to the need for shelter. The pyramid will again develop. Colonnades and perhaps spiral constructions will be raised in useless ostentation of beauty, because the new aesthetics will try to adapt itself to the endless curve of the spiral, which represents the freedom of desire and the triumph of Being in the conquest of infinity. The landscape, brimming with colors and rhythms, will communicate its wealth to the emotions. Reality will be like fantasy. The aesthetics of cloudiness and grays will be seen as the sickly art of the past. A refined and intense civilization will answer to the splendors of a Nature swollen with potency, habitually generous, and shining with clarity. The panorama of present day Rio de Janeiro, or Santos, with the city and the bay, can give us an idea of what the future emporium of the integral race that is to come will be like.

Assuming, then, the conquest of the Tropics by scientific means, there will come a period when all of humanity will establish itself in the warm regions of the planet. The promised land will be, then, in the region that today comprises all of Brazil, plus Colombia, Venezuela, Ecuador, part of Perú, part of Bolivia, and the upper region of Argentina.

There is the danger that science may get ahead of the ethnic process, so that the invasion of the Tropics may take place before the fifth race is completely developed. If this should happen, wars will be waged for the possession of the Amazon, and their outcome will decide the destiny of the world and the fate of the definitive race. If the Amazon is dominated

24

by the English, either of the islands or of the continent, both champions of the pure White, the emergence of the fifth race will remain defeated. But such an outcome would be absurd; History does not bend her ways. The English themselves, would, in the new climate, become more malleable; they would become mestizos, but with them, the process of integration and improvement would be slower. It is preferable then, that the Amazon remain Brazilian, or that it remain Iberian, together with the Orinoco and the Magdalena.[48] With the resources from such region — the richest on earth, filled with all kinds of treasures — the synthetic race will be able to consolidate its culture. The world of the future will belong to whoever conquers the Amazon region. Universopolis will rise by the great river, and from there the preaching, the squadrons, and the airplanes propagandizing the good news will set forth. If the Amazon becomes English, the world metropolis would not be called Universopolis, but Anglotown, and the armies would come out of there to impose upon the other continents the harsh law of domination by the blond-haired Whites and the extinction of their dark rivals. On the other hand, if the fifth race takes ownership of the axis of the future world, then airplanes and armies will travel all over the planet educating the people for their entry into wisdom. Life, founded on love, will come to be expressed in forms of beauty. Naturally, the fifth race will not pretend to exclude the Whites, just as it does not propose to exclude any of the other races. Precisely, the norm of its formation is the use of all capacities for the greater integration of power. Our aim is not war against the Whites, but against any kind of violent domination, be it either by the Whites or, were Japan ever to become a continental danger, by the Yellows. In regards to the Whites and their culture, the fifth race already relies on them, and still expects benefits from their genius. Latin America owes what it is to the white European, and is not going to deny him. To the North Americans themselves, Latin America owes a great part of her railroads, bridges, and enterprises. By the same token, it needs of all the other races. However, we accept the superior ideals of the Whites but not their arrogance. We want to offer them, as well as to all other peoples, a free country where they will find a home and a refuge, but not a continuation of their conquests. The Whites themselves, unhappy with the materialism and social injustice in which their race, the fourth race, has fallen, will come to us for help in this conquest of freedom.

Perhaps the traits of the white race will predominate among the characteristics of the fifth race, but such a supremacy must be result of the free choice of personal taste, and not the fruit of violence or economic pressure. The superior traits of culture and nature will have to triumph, but that triumph will be stable only if it is based on the voluntary acceptance by conscience and on the free choice of fantasy. Up to this date, life has received its character from man's lower faculties; the fifth branch will be the fruit of the superior faculties. The fifth race does not exclude but accumulates life. For this reason, the exclusion of the Yankee, like the exclusion of any other human type, would be equivalent to an anticipated mutilation, more deadly even than a later cut. If we do not want to exclude even the races that might be considered inferior, it would be much less sensible to keep from our enterprise a race full of vigor and solid social virtues.

Now that we have expressed the theory of the formation of the future Ibero-American race, and the manner in which it will be able to take advantage of the environment in which it lives, only the third factor of the transformation which is taking place in our continent remains to be considered: The spiritual factor, which has to direct and consummate this extraordinary enterprise. Some may think, perhaps, that the fusion of the different contemporary races into a new race that will fulfill and surpass all the others is going to be a repugnant process of anarchic hybridization. By comparison, the English practice of marrying only within the same stock may be seen as an ideal of refinement and purity. The primitive Aryans from Hindustan attempted precisely that English system, in order to keep themselves from mixing with the colored races. However, since those dark races possessed a wisdom necessary to complement that of the blond invaders, the true Hindu culture was not produced until after the centuries had completed the mixture, in spite of all written prohibitions. Furthermore, the fateful mixture was useful not only for cultural reasons, but because the physical specimen itself needs to be renovated in its kin. North Americans have held very firmly to their resolution to maintain a pure stock, the reason being that they are faced with the Blacks, who are like the opposite pole, like the antithesis of the elements to be mixed. In the Ibero-American world, the problem does not present itself in such crude terms. We have very few Blacks, and a large part of them is already becoming a mulatto population. The Indian is a good bridge for racial mixing. Besides, the warm climate is propitious for the interaction and gathering of all peoples. On the other hand, and this is essential, interbreeding will no longer obey reasons of simple proximity as occurred in

26

the beginning when the white colonist took an indian or black woman because there were no others at hand. In the future, as social conditions keep improving, the mixture of bloods will become gradually more spontaneous, to the point that interbreeding will no longer be the result of simple necessity but of personal taste or, at least, of curiosity. Spiritual motivation, in this manner, will increasingly superimpose itself upon the contingencies of the merely physical. By spiritual motivation, we should understand, rather than reflective thinking, the faculty of personal taste that directs the mysterious selection of one particular person out of the multitude.

III

On several occasions, I have proposed this law of personal taste as the basis of all human relationships under the name of the law of the three social stages.[49] This is not to be taken in the Comtian sense,[50] but much more comprehensively. The three stages indicated by this law are: The material or warlike, the intellectual or political, and the spiritual or aesthetic. They represent a process that is gradually liberating us from the domination of necessity and, step by step, is submitting all life to the superior norms of feeling and fantasy. In the first stage, only matter rules. Social groups confronting each other either fight or join one another following no other law but violence and relative power. Sometimes, they exterminate each other, or else, they celebrate agreements according to convenience or necessity. This is the way of life typical of the hordes or tribes of all races. In such a situation, the mixing of bloods has also been imposed by material power, which is the only element of cohesion in the group. There can be no selection where the strong take or reject, according to their fancy, the vanquished female.

Of course, even in this period, the instinct of sympathy beats at the core of human relationships, attracting or repelling according to that mystery we call taste, that mystery which is the secret reason for all aesthetics. However, the influence of taste does not constitute the predominant motivation in the first period, nor in the second, which is subjected to the inflexible norms of reason. Reason is also present in the first period as the origin of conduct and human actions, but it is weak, like the suppressed taste. It is not reason that decides but power, and judgment is submitted to that, usually brutal, force, and made into a slave of primitive will. Judgment, thus corrupted into cunning, debases itself in order to serve injustice. In the first period, it is not possible to work towards the cordial fusion of the races. On the one hand, because the law of violence itself, to which this period submits, excludes possibilities of spontaneous cohesion; on the other, because even geographical conditions themselves do not permit the constant communication between all peoples of the earth.

In the second period, reason tends to prevail, artfully making use of the advantages conquered by force and correcting the latter's mistakes. Boundaries are defined by treaties, and customs are organized according to laws derived from reciprocal convenience and logical thinking. Romanism is the most complete model of this rational social system,

28

although it actually started before Rome, and still continues in this time of nationalities. In this system, racial mixing partially obeys the fancy of free instinct, exercised beneath the rigors of the social norm, but more strongly it obeys the ethical and political conveniences of the moment. In the name of morality, for instance, matrimonial ties, difficult to break, are imposed between persons who do not love each other. In the name of politics, internal and external liberties are restricted. In the name of religion, which should be sublime inspiration, dogmas and tyrannies are imposed. Each case is, however, justified with the dictates of reason, recognized as supreme in human affairs. Those who condemn racial mixture in the name of a scientific eugenics which, based on incomplete and false data, has not been able to produce valid results, also proceed according to superficial logic and questionable knowledge. The main characteristic of this second period is faith in the formula. For that reason, in every respect, this period does nothing but give norms to intelligence, limits to action, boundaries to the nation, and reins to the emotions. Rule, norm and tyranny — such is the law of the second period in which we are imprisoned and from which it is necessary to escape.

In the third period, whose approach is already announced in a thousand ways, the orientation of conduct will not be sought in pitiful reason that explains but does not discover. It will rather be sought in creative feeling and convincing beauty. Norms will be given by fantasy, the supreme faculty. That is to say, life will be without norms, in a state in which everything that is born from feeling will be right: Instead of rules, constant inspiration. The merit of an action will not be sought in the immediate and tangible results, as in the first period; nor will it be required to adapt itself to predetermined rules of pure reason. The ethical imperative itself will be surpassed. Beyond good and evil, in a world of aesthetic *pathos*, the only thing that will matter will be that the act, being beautiful, shall produce joy. To do our whim, not our duty; to follow the path of taste, not of appetite or syllogism; to live joy grounded on love — such is the third stage.

Unfortunately, we are so imperfect, that in order to attain such a godly life, it will be necessary that we previously pass through all the paths. First, the path of duty, where the lower appetites are purified and surpassed; then, the path of illusion, that stimulates the highest aspirations. Passion, which redeems lower sensuality, will come immediately afterwards. To live in *pathos*, to feel towards the world an emotion so intense that the movement of things adopts rhythms of joy is a feature of the third period. We arrive at it by letting loose the divine desire, so that it may reach, without moral and logical bridges, in one nimble leap, the realms of revelation. Such immediate intuition that jumps over the chain of sorites is an artistic gift and, being passion, goes beyond duty from the very beginning, and replaces it with exalted love. Duty and logic, it is clear, are the scaffold and the mechanics of building, but the soul of architecture is rhythm, which transcends mechanics and knows no other law but the mystery of divine beauty.

What role is played in this process by the will, that nerve of human destinies that the fourth race even deified in the intoxicating instant of its triumph? Will is power, blind power running after ambiguous ends. In the first period, it is directed by appetite which uses it for all its whims. Then, reason shines her light, the will is refrained by duty and takes shape into logical thinking. In the third period, the will is liberated, it surpasses the finite and explodes and becomes infused with a sort of infinite reality. It fills with rumors and remote purposes. Logic does not suffice and the will takes on the wings of fantasy. It sinks into the deepest and descries the highest. It expands into harmony and ascends into the creative mystery of melody. It satisfies itself and dissolves into emotion, fusing itself with the joy of the universe: It becomes passion of beauty.

If we acknowledge that Humanity is gradually approaching the third period of its destiny, we shall see that the work of racial fusion is going to take place in the Ibero-American continent according to a law derived from the fruition of the highest faculties. The laws of emotion, beauty, and happiness will determine the selection of a mate with infinitely superior results than that of a eugenics grounded on scientific reason, which never sees beyond the less important portion of the love act. Above scientific eugenics, the mysterious eugenics of aesthetic taste will prevail. Where enlightened passion rules, no correctives are necessary. The very ugly will not procreate, they will have no desire to procreate. What does it matter, then, that all the races mix with each other if ugliness will find no cradle? Poverty, defective education, the scarcity of beautiful types, the misery that makes people ugly, all those calamities will disappear from the future social stage. The fact, common today, of a mediocre couple feeling proud of having multiplied misery will seem repugnant then, it will seem a crime. Marriage will cease to be a consolation for misfortunes that need not be perpetuated, and it will become a work of art.

30

As soon as education and comfort become widespread, there will be no danger in the mixture of the most divergent types. Unions will be effected according to the singular law of the third period, the law of sympathy, refined by the sense of beauty; a true sympathy and not the false one that, today, necessity and ignorance impose upon us. Sincerely passionate unions, easily undone in case of error, will produce bright and handsome offspring. The entire species will change its physical makeup and temperament. Superior instincts will prevail and, in a happy synthesis, the elements of beauty apportioned today among different races will endure.

At present, partly because of hypocrisy, and partly because unions are made between miserable persons in an unfortunate state, we see with profound horror the marriage of a black woman and a white man. We would feel no repugnance at all if it were the union of a black Apollo and a blond Venus, which goes to prove that everything is sanctified by beauty. On the other hand, it is repugnant to see those married couples that come out of the judge's office or the temples. They are ugly in a proportion of, more or less, ninety percent of the cases. The world is thus full of ugliness because of our vices, our prejudices, and our misery. Procreation by love is already a good antecedent for a healthy progeny, but it is necessary that love itself be a work of art, and not the last resort of desperate people. If what is going to be transmitted is stupidity, then the ties between the parents is not love, but opprobrious and base instinct.

A mixture of races accomplished according to the laws of social well-being, sympathy, and beauty, will lead to the creation of a type infinitely superior to all that have previously existed. The crossing of opposites, according to Mendel's laws of heredity,[51] will produce discontinuous and quite complex variations, as multiple and diverse as are the elements of human interbreeding. For this reason, such crossing is a guarantee of the limitless possibilities that a well oriented instinct offers for the gradual perfection of the species. If, until now, the human species has not improved greatly, it is because it has lived in conditions of agglomeration and misery which have made impossible the free function of the instinct of beauty. Reproduction has been accomplished in the manner of beasts, with no limit in quantity and no aspiration for improvement. The spirit has not taken part in it, but the appetite that satisfies itself whichever way it can. Thus, we are not in the position even to imagine the modalities and the effects of a series of truly inspired crossings. Unions based on the capability and beauty of the types would have to produce a great number of individuals gifted with the predominant qualities. As a result of choosing quickly, not with reflective thinking but with taste, the qualities we wish to make predominant, the selective types will gradually multiply, while the recessive types will tend to disappear. Recessive offspring would no longer unite among themselves, but in turn would go in search of quick improvement, or would voluntarily extinguish all desire of physical reproduction. The awareness of the species itself would gradually develop an astute Mendelianism, as soon as it sees itself free from physical pressure, ignorance and misery. In this way, in a very few generations, monstrosities will disappear; what today is normal will come to seem abominable. The lower types of the species will be absorbed by the superior type. In this manner, for example, the Black could be redeemed, and step by step, by voluntary extinction, the uglier stocks will give way to the more handsome. Inferior races, upon being educated, would become less prolific, and the better specimens would go on ascending a scale of ethnic improvement, whose maximum type is not precisely the White, but that new race to which the White himself will have to aspire with the object of conquering the synthesis. The Indian, by grafting onto the related race, would take the jump of millions of years that separate Atlantis from our times, and in a few decades of aesthetic eugenics, the Black may disappear, together with the types that a free instinct of beauty may go on signaling as fundamentally recessive and undeserving, for that reason, of perpetuation. In this manner, a selection of taste would take effect, much more efficiently than the brutal Darwinist selection, which is valid, if at all, only for the inferior species, but no longer for man.

No contemporary race can present itself alone as the finished model that all the others should imitate. The mestizo, the Indian, and even the Black are superior to the White in a countless number of properly spiritual capacities. Neither in antiquity, nor in the present, have we a race capable of forging civilization by itself. The most illustrious epochs of humanity have been, precisely, those in which several different peoples have come into contact and mixed with each other. India, Greece, Alexandria, Rome are but examples that only a geographic and ethnic universality is capable of giving the fruits of civilization. In the contemporary period, while the pride of the present masters of the world asserts through the mouth of their scientists the ethnic and mental superiority of the Whites from the north, any teacher can corroborate that the children and youths descendant from

Scandinavians, Dutch, and English found in North American universities, are much slower, and almost dull, compared with the mestizo children and youths from the south. Perhaps this advantage is explained as the result of a beneficial spiritual Mendelianism, caused by a combination of contrary elements. The truth is that vigor is renewed with graftings, and that the soul itself looks for diversity in order to enrich the monotony of its own contents. Only a long lasting experience will be able to show the results of a mixture no longer accomplished by violence, nor by reason of necessity, but by the selection founded on the dazzling produced by beauty and confirmed by the *pathos* of love.

In the first and second periods in which we live, because of isolation and war, the human species lives to a certain extent according to Darwinist laws. The English, who see only the present in the external world, did not hesitate to apply zoological theories to the field of human sociology. If the false translation of physiological law to the realm of the spirit were acceptable, then to speak of the ethnic incorporation of the Black would be tantamount to defending retrogression. The English theory supposes, implicitly or frankly, that the Black is a sort of link nearer the monkey than the blond man. There is no other recourse, for that reason, but to make him disappear. On the other hand, the White, particularly the English-speaking White, is presented as the sublime culmination of human evolution; to cross him with another race would be equivalent to muddling his stock. Such a way of seeing things is nothing but the illusion of each fortunate people during the period of their power. Throughout history, every great nation has thought of itself as the final and chosen one. When these childish presumptions are compared with each other, one can see that the mission each nation attributes to itself is, at the bottom, nothing else but its eagerness for booty and the desire to exterminate the rival power. The official science itself is, in each period, a reflection of the pride of the dominant race. Hebrews grounded the belief in their superiority upon divine oracles and promises. The English base theirs on observations relative to domestic animals. From observations about the crossing and hereditary varieties of such animals, Darwinism gradually emerged, first as a modest zoological theory, and later as a social biology that granted the English definitive preponderance over all the other races. Every imperialistic policy needs a philosophy to justify itself. The Roman Empire proclaimed order, that is, hierarchy: First came the Roman, then his allies, and then the Barbarian under slavery. The

British preach natural selection, with the tacit conclusion that world domination belongs by natural and divine right to the dolichocephalic man from the Isles and his descendants. But this science, which invaded us together with the artifacts of conquering commerce, is fought as all imperialism is fought, by confronting it with a superior science, and with a broader and more vigorous civilization. The truth is that no race suffices by itself and that humanity would stand to lose; it loses each time a race disappears by violent means. It is well and good for each race to transform itself according to its own design, but within its own vision of beauty, and without breaking the harmonious development of human elements. Each ascending race needs to constitute its own philosophy, the *deux ex machina* of its own success. We have been educated under the humiliating influence of a philosophy conceived by our enemies, perhaps innocently if you will, but with the purpose of exalting their own goals and annulling ours. In this manner, even we have come to believe in the inferiority of the mestizo, in the unredemption of the Indian, in the damnation and the irreparable decadence of the Black. Armed rebellion was not followed by a rebellion of the consciences. We rebelled against the political power of Spain and yet did not realize that, together with Spain, we fell under the economic and moral domination of a race that has been mistress of the world since the demise of Spanish greatness. We shook off one yoke to fall under a new one. This displacement to which we fell victims could not have been avoided, even if we had been aware of it sooner. There is a certain fatefulness in the destiny of nations, as well as in the destiny of individuals, but now that a new phase of history has been initiated, it becomes necessary to reconstruct our ideology and organize our continental life according to a new ethnic doctrine. Let us begin, then, by making a new life and a new science. If we do not first liberate the spirit, we shall never be able to redeem matter.

* * *

We have the duty to formulate the basis of a new civilization, and for that very reason, it is necessary that we keep in mind the fact that civilizations cannot be repeated, neither in form nor in content. The theory of ethnic superiority has been simply a means of combat, common to all fighting peoples, but the battle that we must wage is so important that it does not admit any false trickery. We do not claim that we are, nor that we shall become, the first race of the world or the most illustrious, the

34

strongest and the most handsome. Our purpose is even higher and more difficult to attain than temporary selection. Our values are still potential to such an extent that we are nothing yet. However, the Hebrew race was, for the arrogant Egyptians, nothing more than a miserable caste of slaves. Yet, from that race was born Jesus Christ, who announced the love of all men and initiated the greatest movement in history. This love shall be one of the fundamental dogmas of the fifth race that will be produced in America. Christianity frees and engenders life, because it contains universal, not national, revelation. For that reason, it had to be rejected by the Jews themselves, who could not decide to commune with gentiles. But America is the fatherland of gentility, the true Christian promised land. If our race shows itself unworthy of this consecrated land, if it lacks in love, it will be replaced by peoples more capable of accomplishing the fateful mission of those lands, the mission of serving as the seat for a humanity fashioned out of all the nations and all the racial stocks. The bionomy imposed by world progress on the America of Hispanic origin is not a rival creed that confronts the adversary saying: "I surpass you," or "I am self-sufficient." Instead, it is an infinite longing for integration and totality that, for the same reason, invokes the universe. The infinitude of her longing insures her strength to combat the exclusivist creed of the enemy faction and grants her confidence in victory, which always corresponds to the gentiles. The danger is rather that it may happen to us as it happened to the majority of the Hebrews, who, not wanting to become gentiles, lost the grace that originated in their midst. This may happen, if we do not learn how to offer a home and fraternity to all men. Then another people will serve as the axis, another tongue will be the vehicle, but no one can detain any longer the fusion of the races, the emergence of the fifth era of the world, the era of universality and cosmic sentiment.

The doctrine of sociological and biological formation we propose in these pages is not a simple ideological effort to raise the spirits of a depressed race by offering it a thesis that contradicts the doctrine with which its rivals wanted to condemn it. What happens is that, as we discover the falsity of the scientific premise upon which the domination of contemporary power rests, we also foresee, in experimental science itself, orientations that point the way, no longer for the triumph of a single race, but for the redemption of all men. It is as if the palingenesis[52] announced by Christianity with an anticipation of thousands of years, would be confirmed at present by the different branches of scientific knowledge. Christianity preached love as the basis of human relations, and now it begins to be clear that only love is capable of producing a lofty humanity. The official policy and the Positivists' science, which was directly influenced by that policy, said that the law was not love but antagonism, fight, and the triumph of the fittest. However, they established no other criterion to judge fitness, but the curious begging of the question contained in that thesis itself, since the fittest is the one that triumphs, and only the fittest triumph. Thus, we can reduce to verbal formulas of this kind all the small wisdom that wanted to disassociate itself from the genial revelations, in order to substitute them with generalizations founded on the mere sum of details.

* * *

The discredit of such doctrines is aggravated by discoveries and observations that are revolutionizing the sciences today. It was not possible to combat the theory of History as a process of frivolities when it was thought that also individual life was deprived of a metaphysical end and a providential plan. But now mathematics wavers and modifies its conclusions in order to give us the concept of a moveable world, whose mystery changes according to our relative position and the nature of our concepts. Physics and chemistry no longer dare to affirm that the functions of the atom involve nothing else but the action of masses and forces. Biology also states in its new hypotheses, for example, with Uexküll,[53] that in the course of life "cells behave as if they worked within a complete organism whose organs are harmonized according to a plan and work in conjunction, that is, they possess a functional plan . . . there being an interlocking of vital factors in the physico-chemical motor wheel"[54] — a notion which contradicts Darwinism, at least in its interpretation by Darwinists who deny that nature obeys a plan. Mendelianism also demonstrates, according to Uexküll, that the protoplasm is a mixture of substances from which everything, more or less, can be made. Faced with all these changes in the concepts of science, it is necessary to recognize that the theoretical edifice for the domination by a single race has collapsed. This, in turn, is a forewarning that the material power of those who have produced all that false science of circumstance and conquest will not be long in falling.

Mendel's law, particularly when it confirms "the intervention of vital factors in the physico-chemical wheel,"[55] must be part of our new

36

patriotism, because from it we can draw the conclusion that the different faculties of the spirit take part in the processes of destiny.

What does it matter if Spencerian materialism had us condemned, when today it turns out that we can see ourselves as a sort of reserve for humanity, as the promise for a future that will surpass all previous times? We find ourselves, then, in one of those epochs of palingenesis, and in the center of the universal maelstrom. It is urgent to bring to our consciousness all of our faculties in order that, alert and active, they begin to intervene right away in the process of collective redemption. This is the splendid dawn of a peerless age. One could say that it is Christianism that is going to be consummated, now not only in the souls, but at the root of beings. As an instrument for this transcendental transformation, a race has been developing in the Iberian continent; a race full of vices and defects, but gifted with malleability, rapid comprehension, and easy emotion, fruitful elements for the seminal plasma of the future species. The biological materials have already been gathered in abundance: the predispositions, the characters, the genes of which Mendelians speak. Only the organizing impulse, the plan for the formation of the species has been lacking. What should be the traits of this creative drive?

If we were to proceed according to the law of pure confused energy of the first period, according to primitive biological Darwinism, then blind force, by almost mechanical imposition of the most vigorous elements, would make the decision in a simple and brutal manner, exterminating the weak, or, properly speaking, those who do not fit into the plan of the new race. But in the new order, by its own law, the permanent elements will not support themselves on violence but on taste, and, for that reason, the selection will be spontaneous, as it is done by the artist when, from all the colors, he takes only those that are convenient to his work.

If in order to constitute the fifth race we should proceed according to the law of the second period, then a contest of craftiness would ensue, in which the astute ones and those lacking in scruples would win the game over the dreamers and the kind at heart. Probably, then, the new humanity would be predominantly Malaysian, for it is said that no one surpasses them in caution and ability, and even, if necessary, in perfidy. By the road of intelligence, one could even arrive, if you wish, at a humanity of stoics that would take duty as the supreme norm. The world would become like a vast nation of Quakers, where the plan of the spirit would end up strangled and deformed by the rule. Because reason, pure reason, may be able to recognize the advantages of the moral law, but is incapable of imprinting action with the combative ardor to make it fruitful. On the other hand, the joy-creating faculty is contained in the law of the third period, which is a feeling for beauty and a love so refined that it becomes identified with divine revelation. A quality assigned to beauty since ancient times, in the *Phaedro*,[56] for example, is that of being pathetic. Its dynamism is contagious, it moves the emotions and transforms everything, even destiny itself. The race best qualified to discover and to impose such a law upon life and material things will be the matrix race of the new civilization. Fortunately, such a gift, necessary to the fifth race, is possessed in a great degree by the mestizo people of the Ibero-American continent, people for whom beauty is the main reason for everything. A fine aesthetic sensitivity and a profound love of beauty, away from any illegitimate interests and free from formal ties, are necessary for the third period, which is impregnated with a Christian aestheticism that puts upon ugliness itself the redemptive touch of pity which lights a halo around everything created.

We have, then, in the continent all the elements for the new Humanity: A law that will gradually select elements for the creation of predominant types; a law that will not operate according to a national criterion, as would be the case with a single conquering race, but according to a criterion of universality and beauty; and we also have the land and the natural resources. No people in Europe could replace the Ibero-American in this mission, no matter how gifted they might be, because all of them have their culture already made and a tradition that constitutes a burden for such enterprises. A conquering race could not substitute us, because it would fatefully impose its own characteristics, even if only out of the need to exert violence in order to maintain its conquest. This mission cannot be fulfilled either by the peoples of Asia, who are exhausted, or at least, lacking in the necessary boldness for new enterprises.

The people that Hispanic America is forming in a somewhat disorderly manner, yet free of spirit and with intense longings on account of the vast unexplored regions, can still repeat the feats of the Castilian and Portuguese conquerors. The Hispanic race, in general, still has ahead of it this mission of discovering new regions of the spirit, now that all lands have already been explored.

Only the Iberian part of the continent possesses the spiritual factors, the race, and the territory necessary for the great enterprise of initiating the new universal era of Humanity. All the races that are to provide their contribution are already there: The Nordic man, who is today the master of action but who had humble beginnings and seemed inferior in an epoch in which already great cultures had appeared and decayed; the black man, as a reservoir of potentialities that began in the remote days of Lemuria; the Indian, who saw Atlantis perish but still keeps a quiet mystery in the conscience. We have all the races and all the aptitudes. The only thing lacking is for true love to organize and set in march the law of History.

Many obstacles are opposed to the plan of the spirit, but they are obstacles common to all progress. Of course, some people may object, saying that how are the different races going to come to an accord, when not even the children of the same stock can live in peace and happiness within the economic and social regime that oppresses man today. But such a state of mind will have to change rapidly. All the tendencies of the future are intertwined in the present: Mendelianism in biology, socialism in government, growing sympathy among the souls, generalized progress, and the emergence of the fifth race that will fill the planet with the triumphs of the first truly universal, truly cosmic culture.

If we view the process panoramically, we shall find the three stages of the law of the three states of society, each one vivified with the contribution of the four fundamental races that accomplish their mission and, then, disappear in order to create a fifth superior ethnic specimen. This gives us five races and three stages, that is, the number eight which in the Pythagorean gnosis represents the ideal of the equality of all men. Such coincidences are surprising when discovered, although later they may seem trivial.

In order to express all these ideas that today I am trying to expound in a rapid synthesis, I tried, some years ago, when they were not yet well defined, to assign them symbols in the new Palace of Public Education in Mexico. Lacking sufficient elements to do exactly what I wished, I had to be satisfied with a Spanish renaissance building, with two courtyards, archways, and passages that give somewhat the impression of a bird's wing. On the panels at the four corners of the first patio, I had them carve allegories representing Spain, Mexico, Greece, and India, the four particular civilizations that have most to contribute to the formation of Latin America. Immediately below these four allegories, four stone statues should have been raised, representing the four great contemporary races: The white, the red, the black, and the yellow, to indicate that America is home to all and needs all of them.[57] Finally, in the center, a monument should have been raised that in some way would symbolize the law of the three states: The material, the intellectual and the aesthetic. All this was to indicate that through the exercise of the triple law, we in America shall arrive, before any other part of the world, at the creation of a new race fashioned out of the treasures of all the previous ones: The final race, the cosmic race.

LA RAZA CÓSMICA

Misión de la raza iberoamericana

PRÓLOGO

Es tesis central del presente libro que las distintas razas del mundo tienden a mezclarse cada vez más, hasta formar un nuevo tipo humano, compuesto con la selección de cada uno de los pueblos existentes. Se publicó por primera vez[1] tal presagio en la época en que prevalecía en el mundo científico la doctrina darwinista de la selección natural que salva a los aptos, condena a los débiles; doctrina que, llevada al terreno social por Gobineau,[2] dio origen a la teoría del ario puro, defendida por los ingleses, llevada a imposición aberrante por el nazismo.

Contra esta teoría surgieron en Francia biólogos como Leclerc du Sablon[3] y Noüy, que interpretan la evolución en forma diversa del darwinismo, acaso opuesta al darwinismo. Por su parte, los hechos sociales de los últimos años, muy particularmente el fracaso de la última gran guerra,[5] que a todos dejó disgustados, cuando no arruinados, han determinado una corriente de doctrinas más humanas. Y se da el caso de que aun darwinistas distinguidos, viejos sostenedores del spencerianismo,[6] que desdeñaban a las razas de color y las mestizas, militan hoy en asociaciones internacionales que, como la UNESCO, proclaman la necesidad de abolir toda discriminación racial y de educar a todos los hombres en la igualdad, lo que no es otra cosa que la vieja doctrina católica que afirmó la aptitud del indio para los sacramentos y por lo mismo su derecho de casarse con blanca o con amarilla.

Vuelve, pues, la doctrina política reinante a reconocer la legitimidad de los mestizajes y con ello sienta las bases de una fusión interracial reconocida por el Derecho. Si a esto se añade que las comunicaciones modernas tienden a suprimir las barreras geográficas y que la educación generalizada contribuirá a elevar el nivel económico de todos los hombres, se comprenderá que lentamente irán desapareciendo los obstáculos para la fusión acelerada de las estirpes.

Las circunstancias actuales favorecen, en consecuencia, el desarrollo de las relaciones sexuales interraciales, lo que presta apoyo inesperado a la tesis que, a falta de nombre mejor, titulé: de la Raza Cósmica futura.

Queda, sin embargo, por averiguar si la mezcla ilimitada e inevitable es un hecho ventajoso para el incremento de la cultura o si, al contrario, ha de producir decadencias, que ahora ya no sólo serían nacionales, sino mundiales. Problema que revive la pregunta que se ha hecho a menudo el mestizo: ''¿Puede compararse mi aportación a la cultura con la obra de las razas relativamente puras que han hecho la historia hasta nuestros días, los griegos, los romanos, los europeos?'' Y dentro de cada pueblo, ¿cómo se comparan los períodos de mestizaje con los períodos de homogeneidad racial creadora? A fin de no extendernos demasiado, nos limitaremos a observar algunos ejemplos.

Comenzando por la raza más antigua de la Historia, la de los egipcios, observaciones recientes han demostrado que fue la egipcia una civilización que avanzó de sur a norte, desde el Alto Nilo al Mediterráneo. Una raza bastante blanca y relativamente homogénea creó en torno de Luxor un primer gran imperio[7] floreciente. Guerras y conquistas debilitaron aquel imperio y lo pusieron a merced de la penetración negra, pero el avance hacia el norte no se interrumpió. Sin embargo, durante una etapa de varios siglos, la decadencia de la cultura fue evidente. Se presume, entonces, que ya para la época del segundo imperio se había formado una raza nueva, mestiza, con caracteres mezclados de blanco y de negro, que es la que produce el segundo imperio, más avanzado y floreciente que el primero. La etapa en que se construyeron las pirámides, y en que la civilización egipcia alcanza su cumbre, es una etapa mestiza.[8]

Los historiadores griegos están hoy de acuerdo en que la edad de oro de la cultura helénica aparece como el resultado de una mezcla de razas, en la cual, sin embargo, no se presenta el contraste del negro y el blanco, sino que más bien se trata de una mezcla de razas de color claro. Sin embargo, hubo mezcla de linajes y de corrientes.

La civilización griega decae al extenderse el imperio con Alejandro y esto facilita la conquista romana. En las tropas de Julio César ya se advierte el nuevo mestizaje romano de galos, españoles, británicos y aun germanos, que colaboran en las hazañas del imperio y convierten a Roma en centro cosmopolita. Sabido es que hubo emperadores de sangre hispano-romana.[9] De todas maneras, los contrastes no eran violentos, ya que la mezcla en lo esencial era de razas europeas.

Las invasiones de los bárbaros, al mezclarse con los aborígenes, galos, hispanos, celtas, toscanos, producen las nacionalidades europeas, que han sido la fuente de la cultura moderna.

Pasando al Nuevo Mundo, vemos que la poderosa nación estadounidense no ha sido otra cosa que crisol de razas europeas. Los negros, en realidad, se han mantenido aparte en lo que hace a la creación del poderío, sin que deje de tener importancia la penetración

44

espiritual que han consumado a través de la música, el baile y no pocos aspectos de la sensibilidad artística.

Después de los Estados Unidos, la nación de más vigoroso empuje es la República Argentina, en donde se repite el caso de una mezcla de razas afines, todas de origen europeo, con predominio del tipo mediterráneo; el revés de los Estados Unidos, en donde predomina el nórdico.

Resulta entonces fácil afirmar que es fecunda la mezcla de los linajes similares y que es dudosa la mezcla de tipos muy distantes, según ocurrió en el trato de españoles y de indígenas americanos. El atraso de los pueblos hispanoamericanos, donde predomina el elemento indígena, es difícil de explicar, como no sea remontándonos al primer ejemplo citado de la civilización egipcia. Sucede que el mestizaje de factores muy disímiles tarda mucho tiempo en plasmar. Entre nosotros, el mestizaje se suspendió antes de que acabase de estar formado el tipo racial, con motivo de la exclusión de los españoles, decretada con posterioridad a la independencia. En pueblos como Ecuador o el Perú, la pobreza del terreno, además de los motivos políticos, contuvo la inmigración española.

En todo caso, la conclusión más optimista que se puede derivar de los hechos observados es que aun los mestizajes más contradictorios pueden resolverse benéficamente siempre que el factor espiritual contribuya a levantarlos. En efecto, la decadencia de los pueblos asiáticos es atribuible a su aislamiento, pero también, y sin duda, en primer término, al hecho de que no han sido cristianizados.[10] Una religión como la cristiana hizo avanzar a los indios americanos, en pocas centurias, desde el canibalismo hasta la relativa civilización.

I

EL MESTIZAJE

Opinan geólogos autorizados que el continente americano contiene algunas de las más antiguas zonas del mundo. La masa de los Andes es, sin duda, tan vieja como la que más del planeta. Y si la tierra es antigua, también las trazas de vida y de cultura humana se remontan adonde no alcanzan los cálculos. Las ruinas arquitectónicas de mayas, quechuas y toltecas legendarios son testimonio de vida civilizada anterior a las más viejas fundaciones de los pueblos del Oriente y de Europa.[11] A medida que las investigaciones progresan, se afirma la hipótesis de la Atlántida, como cuna de una civilización que hace millares de años floreció en el continente desaparecido y en parte de lo que es hoy América.[12] El pensamiento de la Atlántida evoca el recuerdo de sus antecedentes misteriosos.[13] El continente hiperbóreo desaparecido, sin dejar otras huellas que los rastros de vida y de cultura que a veces se descubren bajo las nieves de Groenlandia; los lemurianos o raza negra del sur; la civilización atlántida de los hombres rojos; en seguida, la aparición de los amarillos, y por último la civilización de los blancos. Explica mejor el proceso de los pueblos esta profunda hipótesis legendaria[14] que las elucubraciones de geólogos como Ameghino,[15] que ponen el origen del hombre en la Patagonia, una tierra que desde luego se sabe es de formación geológica reciente. En cambio, la versión de los imperios étnicos de la prehistoria se afirma extraordinariamente con la teoría de Wegener de la traslación de los continentes.[16] Según esta tesis, todas las tierras estaban unidas, formando un solo continente, que se ha ido disgregando. Es entonces fácil suponer que en determinada región de una masa continua se desarrollaba una raza que después de progresar y decaer era sustituida por otra, en vez de recurrir a la hipótesis de las emigraciones de un continente a otro por medio de puentes desaparecidos. También es curioso advertir otra coincidencia de la antigua tradición con los datos más modernos de la geología, pues, según el mismo Wegener, la comunicación entre Australia, la India y Madagascar se interrumpió antes que la comunicación entre la América del Sur y el Africa. Lo cual equivale a confirmar que el sitio de la civilización lemuriana desapareció antes de que floreciera la Atlántida, y también que el último continente desaparecido es la Atlántida, puesto que las exploraciones científicas han venido a demostrar que es el Atlántico el mar de formación más reciente.

Confundidos más o menos los antecedentes de esta teoría en una tradición tan obscura como rica de sentido, queda, sin embargo, viva la leyenda de una civilización nacida de nuestros bosques o derramada hasta ellos después de un poderoso crecimiento, y cuyas huellas están aún visibles en Chichén Itzá y en Palenque[17] y en todos los sitios donde perdura el misterio atlante. El misterio de los hombres rojos que, después de dominar el mundo, hicieron grabar los preceptos de su sabiduría en la tabla de Esmeralda,[18] alguna maravillosa esmeralda colombiana, que a la hora de las conmociones telúricas fue llevada a Egipto, donde Hermes[19] y sus adeptos conocieron y transmitieron sus secretos.

Si, pues, somos antiguos geológicamente y también en lo que respecta a la tradición, ¿cómo podremos seguir aceptando esta ficción, inventada por nuestros padres europeos, de la novedad de un continente que existía desde antes de que apareciese la tierra de donde procedían descubridores y reconquistadores?

La cuestión tiene una importancia enorme para quienes se empeñan en buscar un plan en la Historia. La comprobación de la gran antigüedad de nuestro continente parecerá ociosa a los que no ven en los sucesos sino una cadena fatal de repeticiones sin objecto. Con pereza contemplaríamos la obra de la civilización contemporánea si los palacios toltecas no nos dijesen otra cosa que el que las civilizaciones pasan sin dejar más fruto que unas cuantas piedras labradas puestas unas sobre otras, o formando techumbre de bóveda arqueada, o de dos superficies que se encuentran en ángulo. ¿A qué volver a comenzar, si dentro de cuatro o cinco mil años otros nuevos emigrantes divertirán sus ocios cavilando sobre los restos de nuestra trivial arquitectura contemporánea? La historia científica se confunde y deja sin respuesta todas estas cavilaciones. La historia empírica, enferma de miopía, se pierde en el detalle, pero no acierta a determinar un solo antecedente de los tiempos históricos. Huye de las conclusiones generales, de las hipótesis trascendentales, pero cae en la puerilidad de la descripción de los utensilios y de los índices cefálicos y tantos otros pormenores, meramente externos, que carecen de importancia si se les desliga de una teoría vasta y comprensiva.

Sólo un salto del espíritu, nutrido de datos, podrá darnos una visión que nos levante por encima de la micro-ideología del especialista. Sondeamos entonces en el conjunto de los sucesos para descubrir en ellos una dirección, un ritmo y un propósito. Y justamente allí donde nada descubre el analista, el sintetizador y el creador se iluminan.

Ensayemos, pues, explicaciones no con fantasía de novelista, pero sí con una intuición que se apoya en los datos de la historia y la ciencia.

La raza que hemos convenido en llamar atlántida prosperó y decayó en América. Después de un extraordinario florecimiento, tras de cumplir su ciclo, terminada su misión particular, entró en silencio y fue decayendo hasta quedar reducida a los menguados imperios azteca e inca, indignos totalmente de la antigua y superior cultura. Al decaer los atlantes, la civilización intensa se trasladó a otros sitios y cambió de estirpes; deslumbró en Egipto; se ensanchó en la India y en Grecia injertando en razas nuevas. El ario, mezclándose con los dravidios,[20]produjo el indostán, y a la vez, mediante otras mezclas, creó la cultura helénica. En Grecia se funda el desarrollo de la civilización occidental o europea, la civilización blanca que al expandirse llegó hasta las playas olvidadas del continente americano para consumar una obra de recivilización y repoblación. Tenemos entonces las cuatro etapas y los cuatro troncos: el negro, el indio, el mogol y el blanco. Este último, después de organizarse en Europa, se ha convertido en invasor del mundo, y se ha creído llamado a predominar, lo mismo que lo creyeron las razas anteriores, cada una en la época de su poderío. Es claro que el predominio del blanco será también temporal, pero su misión es diferente de la de sus predecesores; su misión es servir de puente. El blanco ha puesto al mundo en situación de que todos los tipos y todas las culturas puedan fundirse. La civilización conquistada por los blancos, organizada por nuestra época, ha puesto las bases materiales y morales para la unión de todos los hombres en una quinta raza universal, fruto de las anteriores y superación de todo lo pasado.

La cultura del blanco es emigradora; pero no fue Europa en conjunto la encargada de iniciar la reincorporación del mundo rojo a las modalidades de la cultura preuniversal, representada desde hace siglos por el blanco. La misión trascendental correspondió a las dos más audaces ramas de la familia europea, a los dos tipos humanos más fuertes y más disímiles: el español y el inglés.

* * *

Desde los primeros tiempos, desde el descubrimiento y la conquista, fueron castellanos y británicos, o latinos y sajones, para incluir por una parte a los portugueses y por otra al holandés, los que consumaron la tarea

49

de iniciar un nuevo período de la Historia conquistando y poblando el hemisferio nuevo. Aunque ellos mismos solamente se hayan sentido colonizadores, trasplantadores de cultura, en realidad establecían las bases de una etapa de general y definitiva transformación. Los llamados latinos, poseedores de genio y de arrojo, se apoderaron de las mejores regiones, de las que creyeron más ricas, y los ingleses, entonces, tuvieron que conformarse con lo que les dejaban gentes más aptas que ellos. Ni España ni Portugal permitían que a sus dominios se acercase el sajón, ya no digo para guerrear, ni siquiera para tomar parte en el comercio. El predominio latino fue indiscutible en los comienzos. Nadie hubiera sospechado, en los tiempos del laudo papal que dividió el Nuevo Mundo entre Portugal y España,[21]que unos siglos más tarde ya no sería el Nuevo Mundo portugués ni español, sino más bien inglés. Nadie hubiera imaginado que los humildes colonos del Hudson y del Delaware, pacíficos y hacendosos, se irían apoderando paso a paso de las mejores y mayores extensiones de la tierra, hasta formar la república que hoy constituye uno de los mayores imperios de la Historia.

Pugna de latinidad contra sajonismo ha llegado a ser, sigue siendo, nuestra época; pugna de instituciones, de propósitos y de ideales. Crisis de una lucha secular que se inicia con el desastre de la Armada Invencible y se agrava con la derrota de Trafalgar.[22]Sólo que desde entonces el sitio del conflicto comienza a desplazarse y se traslada al continente nuevo, donde tuvo todavía episodios fatales. Las derrotas de Santiago de Cuba y de Cavite y Manila[23]son ecos distantes pero lógicos de las catástrofes de la Invencible y de Trafalgar. Y el conflicto está ahora planteado totalmente en el Nuevo Mundo. En la Historia, los siglos suelen ser como días; nada tiene de extraño que no acabemos todavía de salir de la impresión de la derrota. Atravesamos épocas de desaliento, seguimos perdiendo no sólo en soberanía geográfica, sino también en poderío moral. Lejos de sentirnos unidos frente al desastre, la voluntad se nos dispersa en pequeños y vanos fines. La derrota nos ha traído la confusión de los valores y los conceptos; la diplomacia de los vencedores nos engaña después de vencernos; el comercio nos conquista con sus pequeñas ventajas. Despojados de la antigua grandeza, nos ufanamos de un patriotismo exclusivamente nacional, y ni siquiera advertimos los peligros que amenazan a nuestra raza en conjunto. Nos negamos los unos a los otros. La derrota nos ha envilecido a tal punto que, sin darnos cuenta, servimos los fines de la política enemiga de batirnos en detalle, de ofrecer ventajas particulares a cada uno de nuestros hermanos, mientras al otro se le sacrifica en intereses vitales. No sólo nos derrotaron en el combate; ideológicamente también nos siguen venciendo. Se perdió la mayor de las batallas el día en que cada una de las repúblicas ibéricas se lanzó a hacer vida propia, vida desligada de sus hermanos (concertando tratados y recibiendo beneficios falsos, sin atender a los intereses comunes de la raza). Los creadores de nuestro nacionalismo fueron, sin saberlo, los mejores aliados del sajón, nuestro rival en la posesión del continente. El despliegue de nuestras veinte banderas en la Unión panamericana[24]de Washington deberíamos verlo como una burla de enemigos hábiles. Sin embargo, nos ufanamos cada uno de nuestro humilde trapo, que dice ilusión vana, y ni siquiera nos ruboriza el hecho de nuestra discordia delante de la fuerte unión norteamericana. No advertimos el contraste de la unidad sajona frente a la anarquía y soledad de los escudos iberoamericanos. Nos mantenemos celosamente independientes respecto de nosotros mismos; pero de una o de otra manera nos sometemos o nos aliamos con la Unión sajona. Ni siquiera se ha podido lograr la unidad nacional de los cinco pueblos centroamericanos, porque no ha querido darnos su venia un extraño y porque nos falta el patriotismo verdadero que sacrifique el presente al porvenir. Una carencia de pensamiento creador y un exceso de afán crítico, que por cierto tomamos prestado de otras culturas, nos lleva a discusiones estériles, en las que tan pronto se niega como se afirma la comunidad de nuestras aspiraciones; pero no advertimos que a la hora de obrar, y pese a todas las dudas de los sabios ingleses, el inglés busca la alianza de sus hermanos de América y de Australia, y entonces el yanqui se siente tan inglés como el inglés en Inglaterra. Nosotros no seremos grandes mientras el español de la América no se sienta tan español como los hijos de España. Lo cual no impide que seamos distintos cada vez que sea necesario, pero sin apartarnos de la más alta misión común. Así es menester que procedamos, si hemos de lograr que la cultura ibérica acabe de dar todos sus frutos, si hemos de impedir que en la América triunfe sin oposición la cultura sajona. Inútil es imaginar otras soluciones. La civilización no se improvisa ni se trunca, ni puede hacerse partir del papel de una constitución política; se deriva siempre de una larga, de una secular preparación y depuración de elementos que se transmiten y se combinan desde los comienzos de la Historia. Por eso resulta tan torpe hacer comenzar nuestro patriotismo con el grito de independencia del padre Hidalgo,[25] o con la conspiración de Quito,[26] o con las hazañas de Bolívar,[27] pues si no lo arraigamos en Cuauhtémoc[28] y en Atahualpa[29] no tendrá sostén, y al mismo tiempo es necesario remontarlo a su fuente hispánica y educarlo en las enseñanzas que deberíamos derivar de las derrotas, que son también nuestras, de las derrotas de la Invencible y de Trafalgar. Si nuestro patriotismo no se identifica con las diversas etapas del viejo conflicto de latinos y sajones jamás lograremos que sobrepase los caracteres de un regionalismo sin aliento universal, y lo veremos fatalmente degenerar en estrechez y miopía de campanario y en inercia impotente de molusco que se apega a su roca.

Para no tener que renegar alguna vez de la patria misma es menester que vivamos conforme al alto interés de la raza, aun cuando ésta no sea todavía el más alto interés de la humanidad. Es claro que el corazón sólo se conforma con un internacionalismo cabal; pero, en las actuales circunstancias del mundo, el internacionalismo sólo serviría para acabar de consumar el triunfo de las naciones más fuertes; serviría exclusivamente a los fines del inglés. Los mismos rusos, con sus doscientos millones de población, han tenido que aplazar su internacionalismo teórico, para dedicarse a apoyar nacionalidades oprimidas como la India y Egipto. A la vez han reforzado su propio nacionalismo para defenderse de una desintegración que sólo podría favorecer a los grandes estados imperialistas. Resultaría, pues, infantil que pueblos débiles como los nuestros se pusieran a renegar de todo lo que les es propio, en nombre de propósitos que no podrían cristalizar en realidad. El estado actual de la civilización nos impone todavía el patriotismo como una necesidad de defensa de intereses materiales y morales, pero es indispensable que ese patriotismo persiga finalidades vastas y transcendentales. Su misión se truncó en cierto sentido con la independencia, y ahora es menester devolverlo al cauce de su destino histórico universal.

En Europa se decidió la primera etapa del profundo conflicto y nos tocó perder. Después, así que todas las ventajas estaban de nuestra parte en el Nuevo Mundo, ya que España había dominado la América, la estupidez napoleónica fue causa de que la Luisiana se entregara a los ingleses del otro lado del mar, a los yanquis, con lo que se decidió en favor del sajón la suerte del Nuevo Mundo. El "genio de la guerra" no miraba más allá de las miserables disputas de fronteras entre los estaditos de Europa y no se dio cuenta de que la causa de la latinidad, que él pretendía representar, fracasó el mismo día de la proclamación del Imperio, por el solo hecho de que los destinos comunes quedaron confiados a un incapaz. Por otra parte, el prejuicio europeo impidió ver que en América estaba ya planteado, con caracteres de universalidad, el conflicto que Napoleón no pudo ni concebir en toda su trascendencia. La tontería napoleónica no pudo sospechar que era en el Nuevo Mundo donde iba a decidirse el destino de las razas de Europa, y al destruir de la manera más inconsciente el poderío francés de la América debilitó también a los españoles; nos traicionó, nos puso a merced del enemigo común. Sin Napoleón no existirían los Estados Unidos como imperio mundial, y la Luisiana, todavía francesa, tendría que ser parte de la Confederación Latinoamericana. Trafalgar entonces hubiese quedado burlado. Nada de esto se pensó siquiera, porque el destino de la raza estaba en manos de un necio; porque el cesarismo es el azote de la raza latina.

La traición de Napoleón a los destinos mundiales de Francia hirió también de muerte al imperio español de América en los instantes de su mayor debilidad. Las gentes de habla inglesa se apoderan de la Luisiana sin combatir y reservando sus pertrechos para la ya fácil conquista de Tejas y California. Sin la base del Misisipi, los ingleses, que se llaman asimismo yanquis por una simple riqueza de expresión, no hubieran logrado adueñarse del Pacífico, no serían hoy los amos del continente; se habrían quedado en una especie de Holanda transplantada a la América, y el Nuevo Mundo sería español y francés. Bonaparte lo hizo sajón.

Claro que no sólo los causas externas, las tratados, la guerra y la política resuelven el destino de los pueblos. Los napoleones no son más que membrete de vanidades y corrupciones. La decadencia de las costumbres, la pérdida de las libertades públicas y la ignorancia general causan el efecto de paralizar la energía de toda una raza en determinadas épocas.

Los españoles fueron al Nuevo Mundo con el brío que les sobraba después del éxito de la Reconquista. Los hombres libres que se llamaron Cortés[30] y Pizarro[31] y Alvarado[32] y Belalcázar[33] no eran césares ni lacayos, sino grandes capitanes que al ímpetu destructivo adunaban el genio creador. En seguida de la victoria trazaban el plano de las nuevas ciudades y redactaban los estatutos de su fundación. Más tarde, a la hora de las agrias disputas con la metrópoli, sabían devolver injuria por injuria, como lo hizo uno de los Pizarro en un célebre juicio. Todos ellos se sentían los iguales ante el rey, como se sintió el Cid, como se sentían los grandes escritores del siglo de oro, como se sienten en las grandes épocas todos los hombres libres.

Pero a medida que la conquista se consumaba, toda la nueva organización iba quedando en manos de cortesanos y validos del monarca. Hombres incapaces, ya no digo de conquistar, ni siquiera de defender lo que otros conquistaron con talento y arrojo. Palaciegos degenerados, capaces de oprimir y humillar al nativo, pero sumisos al poder real, ellos y sus amos no hicieron otra cosa que echar a perder la obra del genio español en América. La obra portentosa iniciada por los férreos conquistadores y consumada por los sabios y abnegados misioneros fue quedando anulada. Una serie de monarcas extranjeros, tan justicieramente pintados por Velázquez[34] y Goya[35] en compañía de enanos, bufones y cortesanos, consumaron el desastre de la administración colonial. La manía de imitar al imperio romano, que tanto daño ha causado lo mismo en España que en Italia y en Francia, el militarismo y el absolutismo trajeron la decadencia en la misma época en que nuestros rivales, fortalecidos por la virtud, crecían y se ensanchaban en libertad.

Junto con la fortaleza material se les desarrolló el ingenio práctico, la intuición del éxito. Los antiguos colonos de Nueva Inglaterra y de Virginia se separaron de Inglaterra, pero sólo para crecer mejor y hacerse más fuertes. La separación política nunca ha sido entre ellos obstáculo para que en el asunto de la común misión étnica se mantengan unidos y acordes. La emancipación, en vez de debilitar a la gran raza, la bifurcó, la multiplicó, la desbordó poderosa sobre el mundo; desde el núcleo imponente de uno de los más grandes imperios que han conocido los tiempos. Y ya desde entonces, lo que no conquista el inglés en las Islas, se lo toma y lo guarda el inglés del nuevo continente.

En cambio, nosotros, los españoles por la sangre o por la cultura, a la hora de nuestra emancipación comenzamos por renegar de nuestras tradiciones; rompimos con el pasado y no faltó quien renegara la sangre diciendo que hubiera sido mejor que la conquista de nuestras regiones la hubiesen consumado los ingleses. Palabras de traición que se excusan por el acto que engendra la tiranía y por la ceguedad que trae la derrota. Pero perder por esta suerte el sentido histórico de una raza equivale a un absurdo, es lo mismo que negar a los padres fuertes y sabios cuando somos nosotros mismos, no ellos, los culpables de la decadencia.

De todas maneras las prédicas desespañolizantes y el inglesamiento correlativo, hábilmente difundido por los mismos ingleses, pervirtió nuestros juicios desde el origen; nos hizo olvidar que en los agravios de Trafalgar también tenemos parte. La ingerencia de oficiales ingleses en los estados mayores de los guerreros de la independencia hubiera acabado por deshonrarnos, si no fuese porque la vieja sangre altiva revivía ante la injuria y castigaba a los piratas de Albión[36] cada vez que se acercaban con el propósito de consumar un despojo. La rebeldía ancestral supo responder a cañonazos lo mismo en Buenos Aires que en Veracruz, en La Habana o en Campeche y Panamá,[37] cada vez que el corsario inglés, disfrazado de pirata para eludir las responsabilidades de un fracaso, atacaba, confiado en lograr, si vencía, un puesto de honor en la nobleza británica.

A pesar de esta firme cohesión ante un enemigo invasor, nuestra guerra de independencia se vio amenguada por el provincialismo y por la ausencia de planes trascendentales. La raza que había soñado con el imperio del mundo, los supuestos descendientes de la gloria romana, cayeron en la pueril satisfacción de crear nacioncitas y soberanías de principado, alentadas por almas que en cada cordillera veían un muro y no una cúspide. Glorias balcánicas soñaron nuestros emancipadores, con la ilustre excepción de Bolívar y Sucre[38] y Petión, el negro,[39] y media docena más, a lo sumo. Pero los otros, obsesionados por el concepto local y enredados en una confusa fraseología seudo revolucionaria, sólo se ocuparon en empequeñecer un conflicto que pudo haber sido el principio del despertar de un continente. Dividir, despedazar el sueño de un gran poderío latino, tal parecía ser el propósito de ciertos prácticos ignorantes que colaboraron en la independencia, y dentro de ese movimiento merecen puesto de honor; pero no supieron, no quisieron, ni escuchar las advertencias geniales de Bolívar.

Claro que en todo proceso social hay que tener en cuenta las causas profundas, inevitables, que determinan un momento dado. Nuestra geografía, por ejemplo, era y sigue siendo un obstáculo de la unión; pero si hemos de dominarlo será menester que antes pongamos en orden al espíritu, depurando las ideas y señalando orientaciones precisas. Mientras no logremos corregir los conceptos, no será posible que obremos sobre el medio físico en tal forma que lo hagamos servir a nuestro propósito.

En México, por ejemplo, fuera de Mina,[40] casi nadie pensó en los intereses del continente; peor aún, el patriotismo vernáculo estuvo enseñando, durante un siglo, que triunfamos de España gracias al valor

55

indomable de nuestros soldados, y casi ni se mencionan las cortes de Cádiz[41]ni el levantamiento contra Napoleón, que electriza la raza, ni las victorias y martirios de los pueblos hermanos del continente. Este pecado, común a cada una de nuestras patrias, es resultado de épocas en que la Historia se escribe para halagar a los déspotas. Entonces la patriotería no se conforma con presentar a sus héroes como unidades de un movimiento continental, y los presenta autónomos, sin darse cuenta que al obrar de esta suerte los empequeñece en vez de agrandarlos.

Se explican también estas aberraciones porque el elemento indígena no se había fusionado, no se ha fusionado aún en su totalidad, con la sangre española; pero esta discordia es más aparente que real. Háblese al más exaltado indianista de la conveniencia de adaptarnos a la latinidad y no opondrá el menor reparo; dígasele que nuestra cultura es española y en seguida formulará objeciones. Subsiste la huella de la sangre vertida, huella maldita que no borran los siglos, pero que el peligro común debe anular. Y no hay otro recurso. Los mismos indios puros están españolizados, están latinizados, como está latinizado el ambiente. Dígase lo que se quiera, los rojos, los ilustres atlantes de quienes viene el indio, se durmieron hace millares de años para no despertar. En la Historia no hay retornos, porque toda ella es transformación y novedad. Ninguna raza vuelve; cada una plantea su misión, la cumple y se va. Esta verdad rige lo mismo en los tiempos bíblicos que en los nuestros; todos los historiadores antiguos la han formulado. Los días de los blancos puros, los vencedores de hoy, están tan contados como lo estuvieron los de sus antecesores. Al cumplir su destino de mecanizar el mundo, ellos mismos han puesto, sin saberlo, las bases de un período nuevo, el período de la fusión y la mezcla de todos los pueblos. El indio no tiene otra puerta hacia el porvenir que la puerta de la cultura moderna, ni otro camino que el camino ya desbrozado de la civilización latina. También el blanco tendrá que deponer su orgullo, y buscará progreso y redención posterior en el alma de sus hermanos de las otras castas, y se confundirá y se perfeccionará en cada una de las variedades superiores de la especie, en cada una de las modalidades que tornan múltiple la revelación y más poderoso el genio.

En el proceso de nuestra misión étnica, la guerra de emancipación de España significa una crisis peligrosa. No quiero decir con esto que la guerra no debió hacerse ni que no debió triunfar. En determinadas épocas el fin trascendental tiene que quedar aplazado; la raza espera, en tanto que la patria urge, y la patria es el presente inmediato e indispensable. Era imposible seguir dependiendo de un cetro que de tropiezo en tropiezo y de descalabro en bochorno había ido bajando hasta caer en las manos sin honra de un Fernando VII.[42] Se pudo haber tratado en las cortes de Cádiz para organizar una libre Federación castellana; no se podía responder a la monarquía sino batiéndole sus enviados. En este punto la visión de Mina fue cabal: implantar la libertad en el Nuevo Mundo y derrocar después la monarquía en España. Ya que la imbecilidad de la época impidió que se cumpliera este genial designio, procuremos al menos tenerlo presente. Reconozcamos que fue una desgracia no haber procedido con la cohesión que demostraron los del norte; la raza prodigiosa, a la que solemos llenar de improperios sólo porque nos ha ganado cada partida de la lucha secular. Ella triunfa porque aduna sus capacidades prácticas con la visión clara de un gran destino. Conserva presente la intuición de una misión histórica definida, en tanto que nosotros nos perdemos en el laberinto de quimeras verbales. Parece que Dios mismo conduce los pasos del sajonismo, en tanto que nosotros nos matamos por el dogma o nos proclamamos ateos. ¡Cómo deben de reir de nuestros desplantes y vanidades latinas estos fuertes constructores de imperios! Ellos no tienen en la mente el lastre ciceroniano de la fraseología, ni en la sangre los instintos contradictorios de la mezcla de razas disímiles; *pero cometieron el pecado de destruir esas razas, en tanto que nosotros las asimilamos, y esto nos da derechos nuevos y esperanzas de una misión sin precedente en la Historia.*

De aquí que los tropiezos adversos no nos inclinen a claudicar; vagamente sentimos que han de servirnos para descubrir nuestra ruta. Precisamente, en las diferencias encontramos el camino; si no más imitamos, perdemos; si descubrimos, si creamos, triunfaremos. La ventaja de nuestra tradición es que posee mayor facilidad de simpatía con los extraños. Esto implica que nuestra civilización, con todos sus defectos, puede ser la elegida para asimilar y convertir a un nuevo tipo a todos los hombres. En ella se prepara de esta suerte la trama, el múltiple y rico plasma de la humanidad futura. Comienza a advertirse este mandato de la Historia en esa abundancia de amor que permitió a los españoles crear una raza nueva con el indio y con el negro; prodigando la estirpe blanca a través del soldado que engendraba familia indígena y la cultura de occidente por medio de la doctrina y el ejemplo de los misioneros que pusieron al indio en condiciones de penetrar en la nueva etapa, la etapa del mundo Uno. La colonización española creó mestizaje; esto señala su carácter, fija su responsabilidad y define su porvenir. El inglés siguió cruzándose sólo con el blanco y exterminó al indigena; lo sigue exterminando en la sorda lucha económica, más eficaz que la conquista armada. Esto prueba su limitación y es el indicio de su decadencia. Equivale, en grande, a los matrimonios incestuosos de la faraones, que minaron la virtud de aquella raza, y contradice el fin ulterior de la Historia, que es lograr la fusión de los pueblos y las culturas. Hacer un mundo inglés; exterminar a los rojos, para que en toda la América se renueve el norte de Europa, hecho de blancos puros, no es más que repetir el proceso victorioso de una raza vencedora. Ya esto lo hicieron los rojos; lo han hecho o lo han intentado todas las razas fuertes y homogéneas; pero eso no resuelve el problema humano; para un objetivo tan menguado no se quedó en reserva cinco mil años la América. El objeto del continente nuevo y antiguo es mucho más importante. Su predestinación obedece al designio de constituir la cuna de una raza quinta en la que se fundirán todos los pueblos, para reemplazar a los cuatro que aisladamente han venido forjando la Historia. En el suelo de América hallará término la dispersión, allí se consumará la unidad por el triunfo del amor fecundo, y la superación de todas las estirpes.

Y se engendrará, de tal suerte, el tipo síntesis que ha de juntar los tesoros de la Historia, para dar expresión al anhelo total del mundo.

Los pueblos llamados latinos, por haber sido más fieles a su misión divina de América, son los llamados a consumarla. Y tal fidelidad al oculto designio es la garantía de nuestro triunfo.

En el mismo período caótico de la independencia, que tantas censuras merece, se advierten, sin embargo, vislumbres de ese afán de universalidad que ya anuncia el deseo de fundir lo humano en un tipo universal y sintético. Desde luego, Bolívar, en parte porque se dio cuenta del peligro en que caíamos, repartidos en nacionalidades aisladas, y también por su don de profecía, formuló aquel plan de federación iberoamericana que ciertos necios todavía hoy discuten.

Y si los demás caudillos de la independencia latinoamericana, en general, no tuvieron un concepto claro del futuro, si es verdad que llevados del provincialismo, que hoy llamamos patriotismo, o de la limitación, que hoy se titula soberanía nacional, cada uno se preocupó no más que de la suerte immediata de su propio pueblo, también es sorprendente observar que casi todos se sintieron animados de un sentimiento humano universal que coincide con el destino que hoy asignamos al continente iberoamericano. Hidalgo, Morelos,[43] Bolívar, Petión el haitiano, los argentinos en Tucumán,[44] Sucre, todos se preocuparon de libertar a los esclavos, de declarar la igualdad de todos los hombres por derecho natural; la igualdad social y cívica de los blancos, negros e indios. En un instante de crisis histórica, formularon la misión trascendental asignada a aquella zona del globo: misión de fundir étnica y espiritualmente a las gentes.

De tal suerte se hizo en el bando latino lo que nadie ni pensó hacer en el continente sajón. Allí siguió imperando la tesis contraria, el propósito confesado o tácito de limpiar la tierra de indios, mogoles y negros, para mayor gloria y ventura del blanco. En realidad, desde aquella época quedaron bien definidos los sistemas que, perdurando hasta la fecha, colocan en campos sociológicos opuestos a las dos civilizaciones: la que quiere el predominio exclusivo del blanco y la que está formando una raza nueva, raza de síntesis, que aspira a englobar y expresar todo lo humano en maneras de constante superación. Si fuese menester aducir pruebas, bastaría observar la mezcla creciente y espontánea que en todo el continente latino se opera entre todos los pueblos y, por la otra parte, la línea inflexible que separa al negro del blanco en los Estados Unidos y las leyes, cada vez más rigurosas, para la exclusión de los japoneses y chinos de California.[45]

Los llamados latinos, tal vez porque desde un principio no son propiamente tales latinos, sino un conglomerado de tipos y razas, persisten en no tomar muy en cuenta el factor étnico para sus relaciones sexuales. Sean cuales fueren las opiniones que a este respecto se emitan, y aun la repugnancia que el prejuicio nos causa, lo cierto es que se ha producido y se sigue consumando la mezcla de sangres. Y es en esta fusión de estirpes donde debemos buscar el rasgo fundamental de la idiosincrasia iberoamericana. Ocurrirá algunas veces, y ha ocurrido ya, en efecto, que la competencia económica nos obligue a cerrar nuestras puertas, tal como lo hace el sajón, a una desmedida irrupción de orientales. Pero, a proceder de esta suerte, nosotros no obedecemos más que a razones de orden económico; reconocemos que no es justo que pueblos como el chino, que bajo el santo consejo de la moral confuciana se multiplican como los ratones, vengan a degradar la condición humana, justamente en los instantes en que comenzamos a comprender que la inteligencia sirve para refrenar y regular bajos instintos zoológicos, contrarios a un concepto verdaderamente religioso de la vida. Si los rechazamos es porque el hombre, a medida que progresa, se multiplica menos y siente el horror del número, por lo mismo que ha llegado a estimar la calidad. En los Estados Unidos rechazan a los asiáticos por el mismo temor del desbordamiento físico propio de las especies superiores; pero también lo hacen porque no les simpatiza el asiático, porque desdeñan y serían incapaces de cruzarse con él. Las señoritas de San Francisco se han negado a bailar con oficiales de la marina japonesa, que son hombres tan aseados, inteligentes y, a su manera, tan bellos como los de cualquiera otra marina del mundo. Sin embargo, ellas jamás comprenderán que un japonés pueda ser bello. Tampoco es fácil convencer al sajón de que si el amarillo y el negro tienen su tufo; también el blanco lo tiene para el extraño, aunque nosotros no nos demos cuenta de ello. En la América latina existe, pero infinitamente más atenuada, la repulsión de una sangre que se encuentra con otra sangre extraña. Allí hay mil puentes para la fusión sincera y cordial de todas las razas. El amurallamiento étnico de los del norte frente a la simpatía mucho más fácil de los del sur, tal es el dato más importante, y a la vez más favorable, para nosotros, si se reflexiona, aunque sea superficialmente, en el porvenir. Pues se verá en seguida que somos nosotros de mañana, en tanto que ellos van siendo de ayer. Acabarán de formar los yanquis el último gran imperio de una sola raza: el imperio final del poderío blanco. Entre tanto, nosotros seguiremos padeciendo en el vasto caos de una estirpe en formación, contagiados de la levadura de todos los tipos, pero seguros del avatar de una estirpe mejor. En la América española ya no repetirá la Naturaleza uno de sus ensayos parciales, ya no será la raza de un solo color, de rasgos particulares, la que en esta vez salga de la olvidada Atlántida; no será la futura ni una quinta ni una sexta raza, destinada a prevalecer sobre sus antecesoras; lo que de allí va a salir es la raza definitiva, la raza síntesis o raza integral, hecha con el genio y con la sangre de todos los pueblos y, por lo mismo, más capaz de verdadera fraternidad y de visión realmente universal.

Para acercarnos a este propósito sublime es preciso ir creando, como si dijéramos, el tejido celular que ha de servir de carne y sostén a la nueva aparición biológica. Y a fin de crear ese tejido proteico, maleable, profundo, etéreo y esencial, será menester que la raza iberoamericana se penetre de su misión y la abrace como un misticismo.

Quizás no haya nada inútil en los procesos de la Historia; nuestro mismo aislamiento material y el error de crear naciones nos ha servido, junto con la mezcla original de la sangre, para no caer en la limitación sajona de constituir castas de raza pura. La Historia demuestra que estas selecciones prolongadas y rigurosas dan tipos de refinamiento físico; curiosos, pero sin vigor; bellos con una extraña belleza, como la de la casta brahmánica milenaria, pero a la postre decadentes. Jamás se ha visto que aventajen a los otros hombres ni en talento, ni en bondad, ni en vigor. El camino que hemos iniciado nosotros es mucho más atrevido, rompe los prejuicios antiguos, y casi no se explicaría si no se fundase en una suerte de clamor que llega de una lejanía remota, que no es la del pasado, sino la misteriosa lejanía de donde vienen los presagios del porvenir.

Si la América latina fuese no más otra España, en el mismo grado que los Estados Unidos son otra Inglaterra, entonces la vieja lucha de las dos estirpes no haría otra cosa que repetir sus episodios en la tierra más vasta y uno de los dos rivales acabaría por imponerse y llegaría a prevalescer. Pero no es esta la ley natural de los choques, ni en la mecánica ni en la vida. La oposición y la lucha, particularmente cuando ellas se trasladan al campo del espíritu, sirven para definir mejor los contrarios, para llevar a cada uno a la cúspide de su destino, y, a la postre, para sumarlos en una común y victoriosa superación.

La misión del sajón se ha cumplido más pronto que la nuestra, porque era más inmediata y ya conocida en la Historia: para cumplirla no había más que seguir el ejemplo de otros pueblos victoriosos. Meros continuadores de Europa en la región del continente que ellos ocuparon, los valores del blanco llegaron al cenit. He ahí por qué la historia de Norteamérica es como un ininterrumpido y vigoroso *allegro* de marcha triunfal.

¡Cuán distintos los sones de la formación iberoamericana! Semejan el profundo *scherzo* de una sinfonía infinita y honda: voces que traen acentos de la Atlántida, abismos contenidos en la pupila del hombre rojo, que supo tanto, hace tantos miles de años, y ahora parece que se ha olvidado de todo. Se parece su alma al viejo cenote[46] maya, de aguas verdes, profundas, inmóviles, en el centro del bosque, desde hace tantos siglos que ya ni su leyenda perdura. Y se remueve esta quietud de infinito, con la gota que en nuestra sangre pone el negro, ávido de dicha sensual, ebrio de danzas y desenfrenadas lujurias. Asoma también el mogol con el misterio de su ojo oblicuo, que toda cosa la mira conforme a un ángulo extraño, que descubre no sé qué pliegues y dimensiones nuevas.

Interviene asimismo la mente clara del blanco, parecida a su tez y a su ensueño. Se revelan estrías judaicas que se escondieron en la sangre castellana desde los días de la cruel expulsión; melancolías del árabe, que son un dejo de la enfermiza sensualidad musulmana; ¿quién no tiene algo de todo esto o no desea tenerlo todo? He ahí al hindú, que también llegará, que ha llegado ya por el espíritu, y aunque es el último en venir parece el más próximo pariente. Tantos que han venido y otros que vendrán, y así se nos ha de ir haciendo un corazón sensible y ancho que todo lo abarca y contiene y se conmueve; pero, henchido de vigor, impone leyes nuevas al mundo. Y presentimos como otra cabeza, que dispondrá de todos los ángulos para cumplir el prodigio de superar a la esfera.

II

Después de examinar las potencialidades remotas y próximas de la raza mixta que habita el continente iberoamericano y el destino que la lleva a convertirse en la primera raza síntesis del globo, se hace necesario investigar si el medio físico en que se desarrolla dicha estirpe corresponde a los fines que le marca su biótica. La extensión de que ya dispone es enorme; no hay, desde luego, problema de superficie. La circunstancia de que sus costas no tienen muchos puertos de primera clase casi no tiene importancia, dados los adelantos crecientes de la ingeniería. En cambio, lo que es fundamental abunda en cantidad superior, sin duda, a cualquiera otra región de la tierra: recursos naturales, superficie cultivable y fértil, agua y clima. Sobre este último factor se adelantará, desde luego, una objeción: el clima, se dirá, es adverso a la nueva raza, porque la mayor parte de las tierras disponibles está situada en la región más cálida del globo. Sin embargo, tal es, precisamente, la ventaja y el secreto de su futuro. Las grandes civilizaciones se iniciaron entre trópicos y la civilización final volverá al trópico. La nueva raza comenzará a cumplir su destino a medida que se inventen los nuevos medios de combatir el calor en lo que tiene de hostil para el hombre, pero dejándole todo su poderío benéfico para la producción de la vida. El triunfo del blanco se inició con la conquista de la nieve y del frío. La base de la civilización blanca es el combustible. Sirvió primeramente de protección en los largos inviernos; después se advirtió que tenía una fuerza capaz de ser utilizada no sólo en el abrigo, sino también en el trabajo; entonces nació el motor, y, de esta suerte, del fogón y de la estufa procede todo el maquinismo que está transformando al mundo. Una invención semejante hubiera sido imposible en el cálido Egipto, y, en efecto, no ocurrió allá, a pesar de que aquella raza superaba infinitamente en capacidad intelectual a la raza inglesa. Para comprobar esta última afirmación basta comparar la metafísica sublime del Libro de los Muertos[47] de los sacerdotes egipcios, con las chabacanerías del darwinismo spenceriano. El abismo que separa a Spencer de Hermes Trimegisto no lo franquea el dolicocéfalo rubio ni en otros mil años de adiestramiento y selección.

En cambio, el barco inglés, esa máquina maravillosa que procede de los vikingos del Norte, no la soñaron siquiera los egipcios. La lucha ruda contra el medio obligó al blanco a dedicar sus aptitudes a la conquista de la naturaleza temporal, y esto precisamente constituye el aporte del blanco a la civilización del futuro. El blanco enseñó el dominio de lo material. La ciencia de los blancos invertirá alguna vez los métodos que empleó para alcanzar el dominio del fuego y aprovechará nieves condensadas, o corrientes de electroquimia, o gases de magia sutil, para destruir moscas y alimañas, para disipar el bochorno y la fiebre. Entonces la humanidad entera se derramará sobre el trópico, y en la inmensidad solemne de sus paisajes las almas conquistarán la plenitud.

Los blancos intentarán, al principio, aprovechar sus inventos en beneficio propio, pero como la ciencia ya no es esotérica no será fácil que lo logren; los absorberá la avalancha de todos los demás pueblos, y finalmente, deponiendo su orgullo, entrarán con los demás a componer la nueva raza síntesis, la quinta raza futura.

La conquista del trópico transformará todos los aspectos de la vida; la arquitectura abandonará la ojiva, la bóveda y, en general, la techumbre, que responde a la necesidad de buscar abrigo; se desarrollará otra vez la pirámide; se leventarán columnatas en inútiles alardes de belleza y, quizá, construcciones en caracol, porque la nueva estética tratará de amoldarse a la curva sin fin de la espiral, que representa el anhelo libre, el triunfo del ser en la conquista del infinito. El paisaje pleno de colores y ritmos comunicará su riqueza en la emoción; la realidad será como la fantasía. La estética de los nublados y de los grises se verá como un arte enfermizo del pasado. Una civilización refinada e intensa responderá a los esplendores de una Naturaleza henchida de potencias, generosa de hábito, luciente de claridades. El panaroma del Río de Janeiro actual o de Santos con la ciudad y su bahía nos pueden dar una idea de lo que será ese emporio futuro de la raza cabal que está por venir.

Supuesta, pues, la conquista del trópico por medio de los recursos científicos, resulta que vendrá un período en el cual la humanidad entera se establecerá en las regiones cálidas del planeta. La tierra de promisión estará entonces en la zona que hoy comprende el Brasil entero, más Colombia, Venezuela, Ecuador, parte de Perú, parte de Bolivia y la región superior de la Argentina.

Existe el peligro de que la ciencia se adelante al proceso étnico, de suerte que la invasión del trópico ocurra antes que la quinta raza acabe de formarse. Si así sucede, por la posesión del Amazonas se librarán batallas que decidirán el destino del mundo y la suerte de la raza definitiva. Si el Amazonas lo dominan los ingleses de las Islas o del continente, que son ambos campeones del blanco puro, la aparición de la quinta raza quedará vencida. Pero tal desenlace resultaría absurdo; la Historia no tuerce sus caminos; los mismos ingleses, en el nuevo clima, se tornarían maleables, se volverían mestizos, pero con ellos el proceso de integración y de superación sería más lento. Conviene, pues, que el Amazonas sea brasileño, sea ibérico, junto con el Orinoco y el Magdalena.[48] Con los recursos de semejante zona, la más rica del globo en tesoros de todo género, la raza síntesis podrá consolidar su cultura. El mundo futuro será de quien conquiste la región amazónica. Cerca del gran río se levantará Universópolis y de allí saldrán las predicaciones, las escuadras y los aviones de propaganda de buenas nuevas. Si el Amazonas se hiciese inglés, la metrópoli del mundo ya no se llamaría Universópolis, sino Anglotown, y las armadas guerreras saldrían de allí para imponer en los otros continentes la ley severa del predominio del blanco de cabellos rubios y el exterminio de sus rivales obscuros. En cambio, si la quinta raza se adueña del eje del mundo futuro, entonces aviones y ejércitos irán por todo el planeta educando a las gentes para su ingreso a la sabiduría. La vida fundada en el amor llegará a expresarse en formas de belleza.

Naturalmente, la quinta raza no pretenderá excluir a los blancos, como no se propone excluir a ninguno de los demás pueblos; precisamente la norma de su formación es el aprovechamiento de todas las capacidades para mayor integración del poder. No es la guerra contra el blanco nuestra mira, pero sí una guerra contra toda clase de predominio violento, lo mismo el del blanco que, en su caso, el del amarillo, si el Japón llegara a convertirse en amenaza continental. Por lo que hace al blanco y a su cultura, la quinta raza cuenta ya con ellos y todavía espera beneficios de su genio. La América latina debe lo que es al europeo blanco y no va a renegar de él; al mismo norteamericano le debe gran parte de sus ferrocarriles y puentes y empresas, y de igual suerte necesita de todas las otras razas. Sin embargo, aceptamos los ideales superiores del blanco, pero no su arrogancia; queremos brindarle, lo mismo que a todas las gentes, una patria libre en la que encuentre hogar y refugio, pero no una prolongación de sus conquistas. Los mismos blancos, descontentos del materialismo y de la injusticia social en que ha caído su raza, la cuarta raza, vendrán a nosotros para ayudar en la conquista de la libertad.

Quizás entre todos los caracteres de la quinta raza predominen los caracteres del blanco, pero tal supremacía debe ser fruto de elección libre del gusto y no resultado de la violencia o de la presión económica. Los caracteres superiores de la cultura y de la naturaleza tendrán que triunfar,

65

pero ese triunfo sólo será firme si se funda en la aceptación voluntaria de la conciencia y en la elección libre de la fantasía. Hasta la fecha, la vida ha recibido su carácter de las potencias bajas del hombre; la quinta rama será el fruto de las potencias superiores. La quinta raza no excluye; acapara vida; por eso la exclusión del yanqui, como la exclusión de cualquier otro tipo humano, equivaldría a una mutilación anticipada, más funesta aún que un corte posterior. Si no queremos excluir ni a las razas que pudieran ser consideradas como inferiores, mucho menos cuerdo sería apartar de nuestra empresa a una raza llena de empuje y de firmes virtudes sociales.

Expuesta ya la teoría de la formación de la raza futura iberoamericana y la manera como podrá aprovechar el medio en que vive, resta sólo considerar el tercer factor de la transformación que se verifica en el nuevo continente; el factor espiritual que ha de dirigir y consumar la extraordinaria empresa. Se pensará, tal vez, que la fusión de las distintas razas contemporáneas en una nueva que complete y supere a todas, va a ser un proceso repugnante de anárquico hibridismo, delante del cual la práctica inglesa de celebrar matrimonios sólo dentro de la propia estirpe se verá como un ideal de refinamiento y de pureza. Los arios primitivos del Indostán ensayaron precisamente este sistema inglés para defenderse de la mezcla con las razas de color, pero como esas razas obscuras poseían una sabiduría necesaria para completar la de los invasores rubios, la verdadera cultura indostánica no se produjo sino después de que los siglos consumaron la mezcla, a pesar de todas las prohibiciones escritas. Y la mezcla fatal fue útil no sólo por razones de cultura, sino porque el mismo individuo físico necesita renovarse en sus semejantes. Los norteamericanos se sostienen muy firmes en su resolución de mantener pura su estirpe; pero eso depende de que tienen delante al negro, que es como el otro polo, como el contrario de los elementos que pueden mezclarse. En el mundo iberoamericano el problema no se presenta con caracteres tan crudos; tenemos poquísimos negros y la mayor parte de ellos se han ido transformando ya en poblaciones mulatas. El indio es buen puente de mestizaje. Además, el clima cálido es propicio al trato y reunión de todas las gentes. Por otra parte, y esto es fundamental, el cruce de las distintas razas no va a obedecer a razones de simple proximidad, como sucedía al principio, cuando el colono blanco tomaba mujer indígena o negra porque no había otra a mano. En lo sucesivo, a medida que las condiciones sociales mejoren, el cruce de sangre será cada vez más espontáneo, a tal punto que no estará ya sujeto a la necesidad, sino al gusto; en último caso, a la curiosidad. El motivo espiritual se irá sobreponiendo de esta suerte a las contigencias de lo físico. Por motivo espiritual ha de entenderse, más bien que la reflexión, el gusto que dirige el misterio de la elección de una persona entre una multitud.

III

Dicha ley del gusto como norma de las relaciones humanas la hemos enunciado en diversas ocasiones con el nombre de la ley de los tres estados sociales,[49] definidos no a la manera comtiana,[50] sino con una comprensión más vasta. Los tres estados que esta ley señala son: el material o guerrero, el intelectual o político y el espiritual o estético. Los tres estados representan un proceso que gradualmente nos va libertando del imperio de la necesidad y, poco a poco, va sometiendo la vida entera a las normas superiores del sentimiento y de la fantasía. En el primer estado manda sólo la materia; los pueblos, al encontrarse, combaten o se juntan sin más ley que la violencia y el poderío relativo. Se exterminan unas veces o celebran acuerdos atendiendo a la conveniencia o a la necesidad. Así viven la horda y la tribu de todas las razas. En semejante situación la mezcla de sangres se ha impuesto también por la fuerza material, único elemento de cohesión de un grupo. No puede haber elección donde el fuerte toma o rechaza, conforme a su capricho, la hembra sometida.

Por supuesto que ya desde ese período late en el fondo de las relaciones humanas el instinto de simpatía que atrae o repele conforme a ese misterio que llamamos el gusto, misterio que es la secreta razón de toda estética; pero la sugestión del gusto no constituye el móvil predominante del primer período, como no lo es tampoco del segundo, sometido a la inflexible norma de la razón. También la razón está contenida en el primer período como origen de conducta y de acción humanas; pero es una razón débil, como el gusto oprimido; no es ella quien decide, sino la fuerza, y a esa fuerza comúnmente brutal, se somete el juicio, convertido en esclavo de la voluntad primitiva. Corrompido así el juicio en astucia, se envilece para servir a la injusticia. En el primer período no es posible trabajar por la fusión cordial de las razas, tanto porque la misma ley de la violencia a que está sometido excluye las posibilidades de cohesión espontánea, cuanto porque ni siquiera las condiciones geográficas permitían la comunicación constante de todos los pueblos del planeta.

En el segundo período tiende a prevalecer la razón que artificiosamente aprovecha las ventajas conquistadas por la fuerza y corrige sus errores. Las fronteras se definen en tratados y las costumbres se organizan conforme a las leyes derivadas de las conveniencias recíprocas y la lógica; el romanismo es el más acabado modelo de este sistema social racional, aunque en realidad comenzó antes de Roma y se prolonga todavía en esta época de las nacionalidades. En este régimen, la mezcla de las razas obedece en parte al capricho de un instinto libre que se ejerce por debajo de los rigores de la norma social, y obedece especialmente a las conveniencias éticas o políticas del momento. En nombre de la moral, por ejemplo, se imponen ligas matrimoniales, difíciles de romper, entre personas que no se aman; en nombre de la política se restringen libertades interiores y exteriores; en nombre de la religión, que debiera ser la inspiración sublime, se imponen dogmas y tiranías; pero cada caso se justifica con el dictado de la razón, reconocido como supremo de los asuntos humanos. Proceden también conforme a lógica superficial y a saber equívoco quienes condenan la mezcla de razas en nombre de una eugénica que, por fundarse en datos científicos incompletos y falsos, no ha podido dar resultados válidos. La característica de este segundo período es la fe en la fórmula; por eso en todos sentidos no hace otra cosa que dar norma a la inteligencia, límites a la acción, fronteras a la patria y frenos al sentimiento. Regla, norma y tiranía, tal es la ley del segundo período en que estamos presos y del cual es menester salir.

En el tercer período, cuyo advenimiento se anuncia ya en mil formas, la orientación de la conducta no se buscará en la pobre razón, que explica pero no descubre; se buscará en el sentimiento creador y en la belleza que convence. Las normas las dará la facultad suprema, la fantasía; es decir, se vivirá sin norma, en un estado en que todo cuanto nace del sentimiento es un acierto. En vez de reglas, inspiración constante. Y no se buscará el mérito de una acción en su resultado inmediato y palpable, como ocurre en el primer período; ni tampoco se atenderá a que se adapte a determinadas reglas de razón pura: el mismo imperativo ético será sobrepujado, y más allá del bien y del mal, en el mundo del *pathos* estético, sólo importará que el acto, por ser bello, produzca dicha. Hacer nuestro antojo, no nuestro deber; seguir el sendero del gusto, no el del apetito ni el del silogismo; vivir el júbilo fundado en amor, esa es la tercera etapa.

Desgraciadamente, somos tan imperfectos que para lograr semejante vida de dioses será menester que pasemos antes por todos los caminos; por el camino del deber, donde se depuran y superan los apetitos bajos; por el camino de la ilusión, que estimula las aspiraciones más altas. Vendrá en seguida la pasión, que redime de la baja sensualidad. Vivir en *pathos*, sentir por todo una emoción tan intensa que el movimiento de las cosas adopte ritmos de dicha, he ahí un rasgo del tercer período. A él se llega soltando el anhelo divino, para que alcance, sin puentes de moral y de lógica, de un solo ágil salto, las zonas de revelación. Don artístico es esa intuición inmediata que brinca sobre la cadena de los sorites y, por ser pasión, supera desde el principio el deber y lo reemplaza con el amor exaltado. Deber y lógica, ya se entiende que uno y otro son andamios y mecánica de la construcción; pero el alma de la arquitectura es ritmo que trasciende el mecanismo y no conoce más ley que el misterio de la belleza divina.

¿Qué papel desempeña en este proceso ese nervio de los destinos humanos, la voluntad que esta cuarta raza llegó a deificar en el instante de embriaguez de su triunfo? La voluntad es fuerza, la fuerza ciega que corre tras de fines confusos; en el primer período la dirige el apetito, que se sirve de ella para todos sus caprichos; prende después su luz la razón, y la voluntad se refrena en el deber y se da formas en el pensamiento lógico. En el tercer período la voluntad se hace libre, sobrepuja lo finito, y estalla y se anega en una especie de realidad infinita; se llena de rumores y de propósitos remotos; no le basta la lógica y se pone las alas de la fantasía; se hunde en lo más profundo y vislumbra lo más alto; se ensancha en la armonía y asciende en el misterio creador de la melodía; se satisface y se disuelve en la emoción y se confunde con la alegría del universo: se hace pasión de belleza.

Si reconocemos que la Humanidad gradualmente se acerca al tercer período de su destino, comprenderemos que la obra de fusión de las razas se va a verificar en el continente iberoamericano conforme a una ley derivada del goce de las funciones más altas. Las leyes de la emoción, la belleza y la alegría regirán la elección de parejas, con un resultado infinitamente superior al de esa eugénica fundada en la razón científica que nunca mira más que la porción menos importante del suceso amoroso. Por encima de la eugénica científica prevalecerá la eugénica misteriosa del gusto estético. Donde manda la pasión iluminada no es menester ningún correctivo. Los muy feos no procrearán, no desearán procrear; ¿qué importa entonces que todas las razas se mezclen si la fealdad no encontrará cuna? La pobreza, la educación defectuosa, la escasez de tipos bellos, la miseria que vuelve a la gente fea, todas estas calamidades desaparecerán del estado social futuro. Se verá entonces repugnante, parecerá un crimen, el hecho hoy cotidiano de que una pareja mediocre se ufane de haber multiplicado miseria. El matrimonio dejará de ser consuelo de desventuras que no hay por qué perpetuar, y se convertirá en una obra de arte.

Tan pronto como la educación y el bienestar se difundan, ya no habrá peligro de que se mezclen los más opuestos tipos. Las uniones se efectuarán conforme a la ley singular del tercer período, la ley de simpatía, refinada por el sentido de la belleza. Una simpatía verdadera y no la falsa que hoy nos imponen la necesidad y la ignorancia. Las uniones, sinceramente apasionadas y fácilmente deshechas en caso de error, producirán vástagos despejados y hermosos. La especie entera cambiará de tipo físico y de temperamento, prevalecerán los instintos superiores y perdurarán, como en síntesis feliz, los elementos de hermosura, que hoy están repartidos en los distintos pueblos.

Actualmente, en parte por hipocresía y en parte porque las uniones se verifican entre personas miserables dentro de un medio desventurado, vemos con profundo horror el casamiento de una negra con un blanco; no sentiríamos repugnancia alguna si se tratara del enlace de un Apolo negro con una Venus rubia, lo que prueba que todo lo santifica la belleza. En cambio, es repugnante mirar esas parejas de casados que salen a diario de los juzgados o los templos, feas en una proporción, más o menos del noventa por ciento de los contrayentes. El mundo está así lleno de fealdad a causa de nuestros vicios, nuestros prejuicios y nuestra miseria. La procreación por amor es ya un buen antecendente de progenie lozana: pero hace falta que el amor sea en sí mismo una obra de arte y no un recurso de desesperados. Si lo que se va a transmitir es estupidez, entonces lo que liga a los padres no es amor, sino instinto oprobioso y ruin.

Una mezcla de razas consumada de acuerdo con las leyes de la comodidad social, la simpatía y la belleza conducirá a la formación de un tipo infinitamente superior a todos los que han existido. El cruce de contrarios, conforme a la ley mendeliana de la herencia,[51]producirá variaciones discontinuas y sumamente complejas, como son múltiples y diversos los elementos de la cruza humana. Pero esto mismo es garantía de las posibilidades sin límites que un instinto bien orientado ofrece para la perfección gradual de la especie. Si hasta hoy no ha mejorado gran cosa es porque ha vivido en condiciones de aglomeración y de miseria en las que no ha sido posible que funcione el instinto libre de la belleza; la reproducción se ha hecho a la manera de las bestias, sin límite de cantidad y sin aspiración de mejoramiento. No ha intervenido en ella el espíritu, sino el apetito, que se satisface como puede. Así es que no estamos en condiciones ni de imaginar las modalidades y los efectos de una serie de cruzamientos verdaderamente inspirados. Uniones fundadas en la capacidad y la belleza de los tipos tendrían que producir un gran número de individuos dotados con las cualidades dominantes. Eligiendo en seguida, no con la reflexión, sino con el gusto, las cualidades que deseamos hacer predominar, los tipos de selección se irán multiplicando, a medida que los recesivos tenderán a desaparecer. Los vástagos recesivos ya no se unirían entre sí, sino a su vez irían en busca de mejoramiento rápido o extinguirían voluntariamente todo deseo de reproducción física. La conciencia misma de la especie irá desarrollando un mendelismo astuto así que se vea libre del apremio físico, de la ignorancia y la miseria, y, de esta suerte, en muy pocas generaciones desaparecerán las monstruosidades; lo que hoy es normal llegará a parecer abominable. Los tipos bajos de la especie serán absorbidos por el tipo superior. De esta suerte podría redimirse, por ejemplo, el negro, y poco a poco, por extinción voluntaria, las estirpes más feas irán cediendo el paso a las más hermosas. Las razas inferiores, al educarse, se harían menos prolíficas, y las mejores especímenes irán ascendiendo en una escala de mejoramiento étnico, cuyo tipo máximo no es precisamente el blanco, sino esa nueva raza a la que el mismo blanco tendrá que aspirar con el objeto de conquistar la síntesis. El indio, por medio del injerto en la raza afín, daría el salto de los millares de años que median de la Atlántida a nuestra época, y en unas cuantas décadas de eugenesia estética podría desaparecer el negro junto con los tipos que el libre instinto de hermosura vaya señalando como fundamentalmente recesivos e indignos, por lo mismo, de perpetuación. Se operaría en esta forma una selección por el gusto, mucho más eficaz que la brutal selección darwiniana que sólo es válida, si acaso, para las especies inferiores, pero ya no para el hombre.

Ninguna raza contemporánea puede presentarse por sí sola como un modelo acabado que todas las otras hayan de imitar. El mestizo y el indio, aun el negro, superan al blanco en una infinidad de capacidades propiamente espirituales. Ni en la antigüedad ni en el presente se ha dado jamás el caso de una raza que se baste a sí misma para forjar civilización. Las épocas más ilustres de la humanidad han sido, precisamente, aquellas en que varios pueblos disímiles se ponen en contacto y se mezclan. La India, Grecia, Alejandría, Roma, no son sino ejemplos de que sólo una universalidad geográfica y étnica es capaz de dar frutos de civilización. En la época contemporánea, cuando el orgullo de los actuales amos del mundo afirma por la boca de sus hombres de ciencia la superioridad étnica y mental del blanco del norte, cualquier profesor puede comprobar que los grupos de niños y de jóvenes descendientes de escandinavos, holandeses e ingleses de la universidades norteamericanas son mucho más lentos, casi torpes, comparados con los niños y jóvenes mestizos del sur. Tal vez se explica esta ventaja por efecto de un mendelismo espiritual benéfico, a causa de una combinación de elementos contrarios. Lo cierto es que el vigor se renueva con los injertos y que el alma misma busca lo disímil para enriquecer la monotonía de su propio contenido. Sólo una prolongada experiencia podrá poner de manifiesto los resultados de una mezcla realizada ya no por la violencia ni por efecto de la necesidad, sino por elección fundada en el deslumbramiento que produce la belleza y confirmada por el *pathos* del amor.

En los períodos primero y segundo en que vivimos, a causa del aislamiento y de la guerra, la especie humana vive en cierto sentido conforme a las leyes darwinianas. Los ingleses, que sólo ven el presente del mundo externo, no vacilaron en aplicar teorías zoológicas al campo de la sociología humana. Si la falsa traslación de la ley fisiológica a la zona del espíritu fuese aceptable, entonces hablar de la incorporación étnica del negro sería tanto como defender el retroceso. La teoría inglesa supone, implícita o francamente, que el negro es una especie de eslabón que está más cerca del mono que del hombre rubio. No queda, por lo mismo, otro recurso que hacerlo desaparecer. En cambio, el blanco, particularmente el blanco de habla inglesa, es presentado como el término sublime de la evolución humana; cruzarlo con otra raza equivaldría a ensuciar su estirpe. Pero semejante manera de ver no es más que la ilusión de cada pueblo afortunado en el período de su poderío. Cada uno de los grandes pueblos de la Historia se ha creído el final y el elegido. Cuando se comparan unas con otras estas infantiles soberbias, se ve que la misión que cada pueblo se atribuye no es en el fondo otra cosa que afán de botín y deseo de exterminar a la potencia rival. La misma ciencia oficial es en cada época un reflejo de esa soberbia de la raza dominante. Los hebreos fundaron la creencia de su superioridad en oráculos y promesas divinas. Los ingleses radican la suya en observaciones relativas a los animales domésticos. De la observación de cruzamientos y variedades hereditarias de dichos animales fue saliendo el darwinismo, primero como una modesta teoría zoológica, después como biología social que otorga la preponderancia definitiva al inglés sobre todas las demás razas. Todo imperialismo necesita de una filosofía que lo justifique; el imperio romano predicaba el orden, es decir, la jerarquía; primero el romano, después sus aliados, y el bárbaro en la esclavitud. Los británicos predican la selección natural, con la consecuencia tácita de que el reino del mundo corresponde por derecho natural y divino al dolicocéfalo de las Islas y sus descendientes. Pero esta ciencia que llegó a invadirnos junto con los artefactos del comercio conquistador se combate como se combate todo imperialismo, poniéndole enfrente una ciencia superior, una civilización más amplia y vigorosa. Lo cierto es que ninguna raza se basta a sí sola, y que la Humanidad perdería, pierde, cada vez que una raza desaparece por medios violentos. En hora buena que cada una se transforme según su arbitrio, pero dentro de su propia visión de belleza y sin romper el desarrollo armónico de los elementos humanos.

Cada raza que se levanta necesita constituir su propia filosofía, el *deus ex machina* de su éxito. Nosotros nos hemos educado bajo la influencia humillante de una filosofía ideada por nuestros enemigos, si se quiere de una manera sincera; pero con el propósito de exaltar sus propios fines y anular los nuestros. De esta suerte nosotros mismos hemos llegado a creer en la inferioridad del mestizo, en la irredención del indio, en la condenación del negro, en la decadencia irreparable del oriental. La rebelión de las armas no fue seguida de la rebelión de las conciencias. Nos rebelamos contra el poder político de España y no advertimos que, junto con España, caímos en la dominación económica y moral de la raza que ha sido señora del mundo desde que terminó la grandeza de España. Sacudimos un yugo para caer bajo otro nuevo. El movimiento de desplazamiento de que fuimos víctimas no se hubiese podido evitar aunque lo hubiésemos comprendido a tiempo. Hay cierta fatalidad en el destino de los pueblos lo mismo que en el destino de los individuos; pero ahora que se inicia una nueva fase de la Historia se hace necesario reconstituir nuestra ideología y organizar conforme a una nueva doctrina étnica toda nuestra vida continental. Comencemos, entonces, haciendo vida propia y ciencia propia. Si no se liberta primero el espíritu, jamás lograremos redimir la materia.

* * *

Tenemos el deber de formular las bases de una nueva civilización, y por eso mismo es menester que tengamos presente que las civilizaciones no se repiten ni en la forma ni en el fondo. La teoría de la superioridad étnica ha sido simplemente un recurso de combate común a todos los pueblos batalladores; pero la batalla que nosotros debemos de librar es tan importante que no admite ningún ardid falso. Nosotros no sostenemos que somos ni que llegaremos a ser la primera raza del mundo, la más ilustrada, la más fuerte y la más hermosa. Nuestro propósito es todavía más alto y más difícil que lograr una selección temporal. Nuestros valores están en potencia, a tal punto que nada somos aún. Sin embargo, la raza hebrea no era para los egipcios arrogantes otra cosa que una ruin casta de esclavos, y de ella nació Jesucristo, el autor del mayor movimiento de la Historia, el que anunció el amor de todos los hombres. Este amor será uno de los dogmas fundamentales de la quinta raza que ha de producirse en América. El cristianismo liberta y engendra vida, porque contiene revelación universal, no nacional, por eso tuvieron que rechazarlo los propios judíos, que no se decidieron a comulgar con gentiles. Pero la América es la patria de la gentilidad, la verdadera tierra de promisión cristiana. Si nuestra raza se muestra indigna de este suelo consagrado, si llega a faltarle el amor, se verá suplantada por pueblos más capaces de realizar la misión fatal de aquellas tierras; la misión de servir de asiento a una humanidad hecha de todas las naciones y todas las estirpes. La biótica que el progreso del mundo impone a la América de origen hispánico no es un credo rival que frente al adversario dice: "te supero, o me basto", sino una ansia infinita de integración y de totalidad que por lo mismo invoca al universo. La infinitud de su anhelo le asegura fuerza para combatir el credo exclusivista del bando enemigo y confianza en la victoria que siempre corresponde a los gentiles. El peligro más bien está en que nos ocurra a nosotros lo que a la mayoría de los hebreos, que por no hacerse gentiles perdieron la gracia originada en su seno. Así ocurriría si no sabemos ofrecer hogar y fraternidad a todos los hombres; entonces otro pueblo servirá de eje, alguna otra lengua será el vehículo; pero ya nadie puede contener la fusión de las gentes, la aparición de la quinta era del mundo, la era de la universalidad y el sentimiento cósmico.

La doctrina de formación sociológica, de formación biológica, que en estas páginas enunciamos, no es un simple esfuerzo ideológico para levantar el ánimo de una raza deprimida ofreciéndole una tesis que contradice la doctrina con que habían querido condenarla sus rivales. Lo que sucede es que, a medida que se descubre la falsedad de la premisa científica en que descansa la dominación de las potencias contemporáneas, se vislumbran también, en la ciencia experimental misma, orientaciones que señalan un camino ya no para el triunfo de una raza sola, sino para la redención de todos los hombres. Sucede como si la palingenesia[52] anunciada por el cristianismo, con una anticipación de millares de años, se viera confirmada actualmente en las distintas ramas del conocimiento científico. El cristianismo predicó el amor como base de las relaciones humanas, y ahora comienza a verse que sólo el amor es capaz de producir una Humanidad excelsa. La política de los estados y la ciencia de los positivistas, influenciada de una manera directa por esa política, dijeron que no era el amor la ley, sino el antagonismo, la lucha y el triunfo del apto, sin otro criterio para juzgar la aptitud que la curiosa petición de principio contenida en la misma tesis, puesto que el apto es el que triunfa y sólo triunfa el apto. Y así, a fórmulas verbales y viciosas de esta índole se va reduciendo todo el saber pequeño que quiso desentenderse de las revelaciones geniales para substituirlas con generalizaciones fundadas en la mera suma de los detalles.

* * *

El descrédito de semejantes doctrinas se agrava con los descubrimientos y observaciones que hoy revolucionan las ciencias. No era posible combatir la teoría de la Historia como un proceso de frivolidades, cuando se creía que la vida individual estaba también desprovista de fin metafísico y de plan providencial. Pero si la matemática vacila y reforma sus conclusiones para darnos el concepto de un mundo movible cuyo misterio cambia de acuerdo con nuestra posición relativa y la naturaleza de nuestros conceptos; si la física y la química no se atreven ya a declarar que en los procesos del átomo no hay otra cosa que acción de masas y fuerzas; si la biología también en sus nuevas hipótesis afirma, por ejemplo, con Uexküll[53] que en el curso de la vida "las células se mueven como si obrasen dentro de un organismo acabado cuyos órganos armonizan conforme a plan y trabajan en común, esto es, posee un plan de función", "habiendo un engrane de factores vitales en la rueda motriz físicoquímica"[54]—lo que contraría el darwinismo, por lo menos en la interpretación de los darwinistas que niegan que la Naturaleza obedezca a un plan—; si también el mendelismo demuestra, conforme a las palabras de Uexküll, que el protoplasma es una mezcla de substancias de las cuales puede ser hecho todo, sobre poco más o menos; delante de todos estos cambios de conceptos de la ciencia, es preciso reconocer que se ha derrumbado también el edificio teórico de la dominación de una sola raza. Esto, a la vez, es presagio de que no tardará en caer también el poderío material de quienes han constituido toda esa falsa ciencia de ocasión y de conquista.

La ley de Mendel, particularmente cuando confirma "la intervención de factores vitales en la rueda motriz físicoquímica",[55] debe formar parte de nuestro nuevo patriotismo. Pues de su texto puede derivarse la conclusión de que las distintas facultades del espíritu toman parte en los procesos del destino.

¿Qué importa que el materialismo spenceriano nos tuviese condenados, si hoy resulta que podemos juzgarnos como una especie de reserva de la humanidad, como una promesa de un futuro que sobrepujara a todo tiempo anterior? Nos hallamos entonces en una de esas épocas de palingenesia y en el centro del *malström* universal, y urge llamar a conciencia todas nuestras facultades, para que, alertas y activas, intervengan desde ya, como dicen los argentinos, en los procesos de la redención colectiva. Esplende la aurora de una época sin par. Se diría que es el cristianismo el que va a consumarse, pero ya no sólo en las almas, sino en la raíz de los seres. Como instrumento de la trascendental transformación, se ha ido formando en el continente ibérico una raza llena de vicios y defectos, pero dotada de maleabilidad, comprensión rápida y emoción fácil, fecundos elementos para el plasma germinal de la especie futura. Reunidos están ya en abundancia los materiales biológicos, las predisposiciones, los caracteres, las *genes* de que hablan los mendelistas, y sólo ha estado faltando el impulso organizador, el plan de formación de la especie nueva. ¿Cuáles deberán ser los rasgos de ese impulso creador?

Si procediésemos conforme a la ley de pura energía confusa del primer período, conforme al primitivo darwinismo biológico, entonces la fuerza ciega, por imposición casi mecánica de los elementos más vigorosos, decidiría de una manera sencilla y brutal, exterminando a los débiles, más bien dicho, a los que no se acomodan al plan de la raza nueva. Pero en el nuevo orden, por su misma ley, los elementos perdurables no se apoyarán en la violencia, sino en el gusto, y, por lo mismo, la selección se hará espontánea, como lo hace el pintor cuando de todos los colores toma sólo los que convienen a su obra.

Si para constituir la quinta raza se procediese conforme a la ley del segundo período, entonces vendría una pugna de astucias, en la cual los listos y los faltos de escrúpulos ganarían la partida a los soñadores y a los bondadosos. Probablemente entonces la nueva humanidad sería predominantemente malaya, pues se asegura que nadie les gana en cautela y habilidad y aun, si es necesario, en perfidia. Por el camino de la inteligencia se podría llegar aún, si se quiere, a una humanidad de estoicos que adoptara como norma suprema el deber. El mundo se volvería como un vasto pueblo de cuáqueros, en donde el plan del espíritu acabaría por sentirse estrangulado y contrahecho por la regla. Pues la razón, la pura razón, puede reconocer las ventajas de la ley moral, pero no es capaz de imprimir a la acción el ardor combativo que la vuelve fecunda. En cambio, la verdadera potencia creadora de júbilo está contenida en la ley del tercer período, que es emoción de belleza y un amor tan acendrado que se confunde con la revelación divina. Propiedad de antiguo señalada a la belleza, por ejemplo en el *Fedro*,[56] es la de ser patética; su dinamismo contagia y mueve los ánimos, transforma las cosas y el mismo destino. La raza más apta para adivinar y para imponer semejante ley en la vida y en las cosas, esa será la raza matriz de la nueva era de civilización. Por fortuna, tal don, necesario a la quinta raza, lo posee en grado subido la gente mestiza del continente iberoamericano; gente para quien la belleza es la razón mayor de toda cosa. Una fina sensibilidad estética y un amor de belleza profunda ajenos a todo interés bastardo y libre de trabas formales, todo eso es necesario al tercer período impregnado de esteticismo cristiano que sobre la misma fealdad pone el toque redentor de la piedad que enciende un halo alrededor de todo lo creado.

Tenemos, pues, en el continente todos los elementos de la nueva humanidad; una ley que irá seleccionando factores para la creación de tipos predominantes, ley que operará no conforme a criterio nacional, como tendría que hacerlo una sola raza conquistadora, sino con criterio de universalidad y belleza; y tenemos también el territorio y los recursos naturales. Ningún pueblo de Europa podría reemplazar al iberoamericano en esta misión, por bien dotado que esté, pues todos tienen su cultura ya hecha y una tradición que para obras semejantes constituye un peso. No podría substituirnos una raza conquistadora, porque fatalmente impondría sus propios rasgos, aunque sólo sea por la necesidad de ejercer la violencia para mantener su conquista. No pueden llenar esta misión universal tampoco los pueblos del Asia, que están exhaustos o, por lo menos, faltos del arrojo necesario a las empresas nuevas.

La gente que está formando la América hispánica, un poco desbaratada, pero libre de espíritu y con el anhelo en tensión a causa de las grandes regiones inexploradas, puede todavía repetir las proezas de los conquistadores castellanos y portugueses. La raza hispánica en general tiene todavía por delante esta misión de descubrir nuevas zonas en el espíritu, ahora que todas las tierras están exploradas.

Solamente la parte ibérica del continente dispone de los factores espirituales, la raza y el territorio que son necesarios para la gran empresa de iniciar la era universal de la humanidad. Están allí todas las razas que han de ir dando su aporte; el hombre nórdico, que hoy es maestro de acción, pero que tuvo comienzos humildes y parecía inferior en una época en que ya habían aparecido y decaído varias grandes culturas; el negro, como una reserva de potencialidades que arrancan de los días remotos de la Lemuria; el indio, que vio perecer la Atlántida, pero guarda un quieto misterio en la conciencia; tenemos todos los pueblos y todas las aptitudes, y sólo hace falta que el amor verdadero organice y ponga en marcha la ley de la Historia.

Muchos obstáculos se oponen al plan del espíritu, pero son obstáculos comunes a todo progreso. Desde luego ocurre objetar que cómo se van a unir en concordia las distintas razas si ni siquiera los hijos de una misma estirpe pueden vivir en paz y alegría dentro del régimen económico y social que hoy oprime a los hombres. Pero tal estado de los ánimos tendrá que cambiar rápidamente. Las tendencias todas del futuro se entrelazan en la actualidad: mendelismo en biología, socialismo en el gobierno, simpatía creciente en las almas, progreso generalizado y aparición de la quinta raza que llenará el planeta, con los triunfos de la primera cultura verdaderamente universal, verdaderamente cósmica.

Si contemplamos el proceso en panorama, nos encontraremos con las tres etapas de la ley de los tres estados de la sociedad, vivificadas cada una con el aporte de las cuatro razas fundamentales que consuman su misión y en seguida desaparecen para crear un quinto tipo étnico superior. Lo que da cinco razas y tres estados, o sea el número ocho, que en la gnosis pitagórica representa el ideal de la igualdad de todos los hombres. Semejantes coincidencias o aciertos sorprenden cuando se les descubre, aunque después parezcan triviales.

Para expresar todas estas ideas que hoy procuro exponer en rápida síntesis, hace algunos años, cuando todavía no se hallaban bien definidas, procuré darles signos en el nuevo Palacio de la Educación Pública de México. Sin elementos bastantes para hacer exactamente lo que deseaba, tuve que conformarme con una construcción renacentista española, de

dos patios, con arquerías y pasarelas, que tienen algo de la impresión de
un ala. En los tableros de los cuatro ángulos del patio anterior hice labrar
alegorías de España, de México, Grecia y la India, las cuatro
civilizaciones particulares que más tienen que contribuir a la formación
de la América latina. En seguida, debajo de estas cuatro alegorías
debieron levantarse cuatro grandes estatuas de piedra de las cuatro
grandes razas contemporáneas: la blanca, la roja, la negra y la amarilla,
para indicar que la América es hogar de todas y de todas necesita.[57]
Finalmente, en el centro debía erigirse un monumento que en alguna
forma simbolizara la ley de los tres estados: el material, el intelectual y el
estético. Todo para indicar que mediante el ejercicio de la triple ley
llegaremos en América, antes que en parte alguna del globo, a la creación
de una raza hecha con el tesoro de todas las anteriores, la raza final, la
raza cósmica.

Notes to *The Cosmic Race* / *La raza cósmica*

[1] Vasconcelos refers here to the first edition (1925) of *La raza cósmica*.

[2] Joseph Arthur, Comte de Gobineau (1816-1882). French diplomat and man of letters. His most famous work was *Essai sur L'inegalite des races humaines* (Paris, 1853-1855), in which he develops a racial theory of history, based on the principle that human races are innately unequal and that the white races, especially the Aryans, are innately superior. He argues that races can change their character only by intermixture, and that degeneration derives from excessive interbreeding between the white and other races. Gobineau exercised considerable influence on German writers, such as Taine and Nietzsche, and his racial theories had particularly deep influence in Germany because they seemed to favor a Pangermanist ideology. Vasconcelos seems to borrow from Gobineau the idea of the struggle between Aryans and Latins which appears further on in this essay, as indicated by N. F. Juárez in his thesis, "Jose Vasconcelos' Theory of the Cosmic Race" (UCLA, Los Angeles, 1965), p. 27.

[3] Albert Mathieu Leclerc du Sablon (1859-1944). French botanist, author of a *Cours de botanique* (1900) and a *Traite de physiology et agricole* (Paris, 1911).

[4] Pierre Lecomte du Noüy (1883-1947). French biologist, author, among other works, of *Le Temps e la Vié* (1936), *L'Avenir de l'espirit* (1942), *L'Homme et sa destinée* (1948).

[5] World War II.

[6] From Herbert Spencer (1820-1903). English philosopher. His "System of Synthetic Philosophy," developed between 1862 and 1893 in a series of works ranging from First Principles to Biology, Psychology, Sociology and Ethics, has as its basis the idea of evolution, characterized as an increasing differentiation and individuation, and an increasing interdependence. While Darwinism applied the theory of evolution only to an explanation of the origin of species, Spencerianism considered evolution the fundamental law of the universe, and seemed to reduce all human phenomena to the materialistic explanations of science. Like

Darwinism, it was used to justify the political supremacy of the so-called white races over the others, as well as the economic exploitation of the latter, by assigning biological superiority to those races that appeared to be more efficient and culturally developed in the contemporary period. Taking the idea of evolution to the social and political level, Spencer argued (in *The Man versus the State*, 1884) for complete individual freedom and individual rights, since freedom provided the conditions of progress by elimination of the unfit, while state intervention preserved the unfit and led to stagnation.

Vasconcelos may have been influenced by Spencer in his attempt to develop a comprehensive system of philosophy that would synthesize the accomplishments of science, religion, and art. He may have also borrowed from Spencer the idea, which appears further on in this essay, of the transformation of society from a military to an industrialist society. In the former, society is held together by force and status, while in the latter, where all men are ends in themselves, contract is the basis of human relationships (*Chambers*, 1973, Vol. 13, pp. 83-84).

[7] Religious and cultural complex near Thebes, ancient capital of Upper Egypt. The temple of Luxor was begun during the 18th Dynasty, which marks the beginning of the New Empire, by Amenhotep III, the Magnificent (1417-1479 B.C.), the ruling Pharaoh when the Exodus of the Hebrew people took place.

[8] Vasconcelos' chronology seems somewhat confused, and even reversed, since the construction of the pyramids precedes by many centuries the building of Luxor. The age of the great pyramid builders was the 4th Dynasty (c. 2613-2494 B.C.), during the period called the Old Kingdom, centuries before the beginning of the Theban dynasties, which mark the predominance of Luxor.

There is no question, however, that Egyptian civilization was the product of a mixed race, with a greater mixture of negroid blood in the population of the south (Upper Egypt) and of Mediterranean stock in the north (Lower Egypt). The Lybians, on the western side of the Nile, were fair and blue-eyed; the Nubians, to the south, were dark with slightly negroid features; while further south were the Blacks of Central Africa. The latter intermarried with the Nubians, while the fairer types with reddish hair occasionally depicted in the murals may be due, it has been suggested, to intermarriage with the Lybians. That ancient Egyptians were a fully mixed race is shown by the fact that "physical anthropologists can see no significant difference between skull measurements of dynastic Egyptians from cemeteries in various parts of Egypt." (*Britannica,* 1971, Vol. 8, p. 41).

[9] Trajan (98-117 A.D.), Hadrian (117-138 A.D.), probably Marcus Aurelius (151-180 A.D.), and Theodosius I (347-395). Also of Spanish origin were the writers Seneca, Lucan, Martial, and Quintilian.

[10] This statement of Vasconcelos is surprising in view of the fact that he was acquainted with and admired Oriental thought and religious concepts (see his *Estudios indostánicos,* 1916), except that his view was colored by Western interpretations of Indian thought as decadent and apathetic. For Vasconcelos, Christianity, as the religion of love, represents an advance over Buddhism as the religion of nirvana (interpreted as dissolution into nothing). For a discussion of Western difficulties with this term, see Trevor Ling, *A History of Religion East or West,* (New York, Harper, 1968) pp. 91-95.

[11] According to scientific data, urban civilization in the Old World can be traced back to the third and second millenium B.C., approximately 2740 B.C. in Egypt, 2000 B.C. in Mesopotamia, and 2000 B.C. in India; in America, however, the Maya civilization can be traced only as far back as 292 A.D. and the Inca to 1200 A.D. Vasconcelos' statement makes sense only if we take into account theories such as those put forth by the Theosophists (see note 13), which trace Maya, Quechua, and Toltec cultures to Atlantean origins, millions of years B.C. Needless to say, no scientific basis for such theories exists, or is claimed.

[12] It is difficult to determine to what "research" Vasconcelos was referring, although at the beginning of the XX century the existence of Atlantis was still a much debated issue. In 1912, the publication, in the *New York American,* of an article titled "How I Discovered Atlantis, the Source of All Civilization," by Paul Schliemann, caused a great stir. The author revealed the possession of a bronze vase and other artifacts discovered by his father, world famous archeologist, Heinrich Schliemann, in the excavations of Troy, and inscribed with the legend,

"From King Cronos of Atlantis." The article promised a forthcoming book on the subject, however, neither the book nor the artifacts ever appeared and the author was discredited. Yet, as late as 1928, Schliemann's article was still cited as trustworthy in a book by José Barbero Garrido, *El misterio de la Atlántida* (Madrid, 1928).

[13] Vasconcelos' allusion to the "mysterious" continents, predecessors of Atlantis, originates in the ideas of the Theosophists, the occultist movement founded by Helena P. Blavatsky (1831-1891), author of, among other books, a six volume work, *The Secret Doctrine: The Synthesis of Science, Religion, and Philosophy* (Adyar: Theosoph. Pub. House, 1888-1936). The title alone suggests Vasconcelos' attempt at a philosophical synthesis of the different branches of intellectual and spiritual knowledge.

That Vasconcelos was familiar with Theosophical writings, as well as with their discredit in scientific circles, is clearly indicated by his commentaries in *Estudios indostánicos* (*O.C.*, Vol. III, p. 328) and in his autobiography. Referring to his first visit to New York in 1916, Vasconcelos reminisces in *Ulises criollo*: "Allí empecé las lecturas indostánicas de Max Müller y Oldenberg, sin omitir el caos teosófico de la Blavatsky y la Bessant. La confusión de estas últimas me dio la idea de tomar notas que más tarde se convirtieron en mi libro, *Estudios indostánicos*, destinado a combatir las falsificaciones" (*O.C.*, Vol. I, p. 611). Again, in *La tormenta,* referring to his stay in San Diego, California, where he finished his *Estudios indostánicos*, Vasconcelos writes, "lo esencial estaba en la tarea que me aguardaba: poner orden en el caudal de ideas que los teósofos a lo Blavatsky volvían confusión . . ." (*O.C.*, Vol. 1, p. 1172).

Yet, in this introductory paragraph to *La raza cósmica*, Vasconcelos evidently makes use of Theosophist cosmogony. According to Blavatsky, Humanity has evolved in seven stages or cycles, each characterized by a different race. The first race, a sort of astral body, inhabited the "Imperishable Sacred Land". The second race inhabited the Hyperborean continent in the Arctic. The third race was the Lemurian, hermaphrodites, inhabitants of the lost Lemuria, the sunken continent that joined South Africa and India. The fourth race was the Atlantean, very similar to the present human races. The fifth race is the present day Human, while the sixth and seventh races are still to come. (L. Sprague de Camp, *Lost Continents: The Atlantis Theme in History, Science and Literature*. New York: Dover, 1970, pp. 51-57.)

This evolutionary scheme was more or less followed and elaborated upon by other Theosophists. It is interesting to note, for instance, W. Scott-Elliot's description of the Toltecs, one of the Atlantean sub-races, in *The Story of Atlantis and the Lost Lemuria* (London: Theosoph. Pub. House, 1896-1926): "So dominant and so endowed with vitality was this race that intermarriages with the following sub-races failed to modify the type, which still remained Toltec; and hundreds of thousands of years later we find one of their remote family races ruling magnificently in Mexico and Peru, long ages before their degenerate descendants were conquered by the fiercer Aztec tribes from the north" (As quoted by James Bramwell, *Lost Atlantis*. New York: Freeway Press, 1973, p. 199).

However, Vasconcelos' summary mentions only four races and is closer to one found in Edouard Schuré, whose work, *The Great Initiates* (Paris, 1889) attained popularity in Latin America, especially in Argentina and Mexico. He writes:

"The four races which share the globe today are daughters of varied lands.

The southern continent, engulfed by the last great flood, was the cradle of the primitive red race of which the American Indians are but remnants, descended from the troglodytes, who reached the top of the mountains when their continent sank. Africa is the mother of the black race, called the Ethiopian by the Greeks. Asia gave birth to the yellow race, preserved in the Chinese. The last arrival, the white race, came from the forests of Europe, between the tempests of the Atlantic and the laughter of the Mediterranean. All human types are the result of mixtures, combinations, degeneracies or selections of these four great races. In the preceding cycles, red and black races rule successively with powerful civilizations which have left traces in Cyclopean structures as well as in the architecture of Mexico. The temples of India and Egypt had traditions concerning these vanished civilizations. — In our cycle the white race is predominant . . . .

85

According to Brahmanic traditions, civilization probably began on our globe five thousand years ago, with the red race on the southern continent, while all of Europe and part of Asia were still under water . . . . The red race, as we have said, inhabited the southern continent, now engulfed, called *Atlantis* by Plato, in keeping with Egyptian traditions . . . . Several Polynesian races, as well as the Indians of North America and the Aztecs whom the Spanish conquerors found in Mexico, are the survivors of this ancient red race whose civilization, lost forever, had its days of glory and material splendor. All these people carry in their souls the incurable melancholy of old races which die without hope. (*The Ancient Mysteries of the East*. New York: Multimedia Publishing Corp., 1973, pp. 36-37).

[14] The Barcelona edition (Agencia Mundial de Librería, 192?) reads here "oculista," obviously a misprint for "ocultista."

[15] Florentino Ameghino (1854-1911). Argentinian paleontologist. One of his contentions was that all mammals of the world, including man, had their origin in Argentina and the South American continent.

[16] Alfred L. Wegener (1880-1930). German geophysicist, author of the theory of the translation of continents, expounded in his work, *The Origin of Continents and Oceans* (1915; translated into Spanish in 1924). The theory presumes the existence of a super-continent, "Panagaea," during the Paleozoic period, from which continental land masses broke off and drifted apart, giving origin to present day continents. One of the bases for Wegener's theory is the fact that the outline of the coasts of different continents match each other like a jigsaw puzzle, as it is noticeable, for instance, in the Atlantic coasts of South America and Africa. This theory has received greater support from recent studies of the Earth's crust and sediment at the bottom of the oceans. (See Samuel W. Mathews, "This Changing Earth". *National Geographic*, Vol. 143, No. 1, Jan. 1973, pp. 1-37).

Vanconcelos' contention, that this theory supports the idea of the existence of Atlantis, seems questionable, since, to the scientific theory, the separation of the continents was completed during the Pleistocene, long before the appearance of human civilizations. On the other hand,

Theosophists and Anthroposophists date the origin of pre-human races in millions of years, and the age of Atlantis from 75000 to the date of the last catastrophe in 9564 B.C. (Bramwell, op, cit., pp. 193-195).

[17] Chichén Itzá and Palenque. Maya ruins in Yucatan and southern Mexico whose art and decorations are strikingly reminiscent of Indian and Egyptian art and architecture. The origin and decline of the Maya civilization still remains a mystery.

[18] The *Emerald Table*: Famous alchemical text of the Middle Ages, first translated from Arabic to Latin at about 1144 by Hugh of Santalla. Early references to it are found in the work Albertus Magnus, *de Mineralibus*, and in Roger Bacon's *Secretum Secretorum*. It is a brief summary of the principles of change in Nature, the foundations of alchemical doctrine, which purports to have been found on a plaque of emerald in the hands of the corpse of Hermes Trismegistus by Galienus Alfachim (or the Physician). There are several versions of it in Arabic, and their divergence is wide enough to make it probable that its ultimate origin must be sought, before the Islamic invasion, in Alexandrian philosophy, when Egypt was still Christian, though with Pagan elements.

As for the term emerald, it was used by Egyptians and Greeks not only for the true beryl, but also for any green substance such as green granite and green jasper. In Medieval times, green glass was referred to as emerald, like the emerald tables of the Gothic kings of Spain.

The opening sentences of the *Table* which may suggest chemical principles as well as a mystic esoteric doctrine, read as follows:

> What is above is like what is below, and what is below is like what is above to effect the miracles of one thing.
> And as all things were by contemplation of one, so all things arose from this one thing by a single act of adaptation.
> The father thereof is the Sun, the mother the Moon.
> The wind carried it in its womb, the earth is the nurse thereof.
> It is the father of all works of wonder throughout the whole world.
> The power thereof is perfect.
> If it be cast on the earth, it will separate the element of earth from that of fire, the subtle from the gross.

With great sagacity it doth ascend gently from earth to heaven.

Again it doth descend to earth, and uniteth in itself the force from things superior and things inferior.

Thus thou will possess the glory of the brightness of the whole world, and obscurity will fly far from thee.

This thing is the strong fortitude of all strength for it overcometh every subtle thing and doth penetrate every solid substance.

Thus was the world created.

Hence will there be marvelous adaptations achieved, of which the manner is this.

For this reason I am called Hermes Trismegistus, because I hold three parts of the wisdom of the whole world.

That which I had to say about the operation of Sol is completed. (See Robert Steele and Dorothea Waley Singer, "The Emerald Table," *Proceedings of the Royal Society of Medicine, Historical section*. Jan. 1928, Vol. 21, part 1, pp. 485-501. For more complete reference, see Julius Ruska, Tabula Smaragdina, Heidelberg, 1926.).

In freemasonry, the *Emerald Table* refers to the revelation of God to man (*Dictionary of Mythology, Folklore and Symbols*. New York, 1961, p. 509).

[19] Hermes Trismegistus (Hermes Thrice-Great). Mythical-historical character identified with Greek god Hermes (Mercury), and with Egyptian god Thoth. According to Cicero, Mercury was expelled from his country after killing Argos and went to Egypt, where he established new laws and taught new arts to the inhabitants, who named him Thoth. Many and diverse discoveries were attributed to him, such as mathematics, algebra, geometry, the game of dice, writing and the alphabet. (The emblem of medicine — a staff with two snakes and a winged hat — known as the caduceus of Hermes, is an ancient symbol which alludes to the Hermetic origin of this science). Many books, as well, were attributed to him, up to 37, 525 by some counts; the so-called "Hermetic" writings. These are of two kinds: 1) Greek and Latin writings, such as the

Poimandres, collectively known as the *Corpus Hermeticum*, which contain religious and philosophical teachings, somewhat related to Gnosticism, and probably dating from the first three centuries A.D. 2) Writings concerning astrology, magic, alchemy (such as the *Emerald Table*) and kindred forms of pseudoscience and occult arts. It is this latter connection which accounts for the frequent references to Hermes Trismegistus in Medieval and Renaissance literature. (See *Hermetica*. Ed. and tr. by Walter Scott, Oxford, 1924).

In order to understand Vasconcelos' great admiration for this mythical figure, it is interesting to note the relationship of the "popular" Hermetic literature with ideas and beliefs about the Cosmos which were widely held in the early Roman empire; ideas which somewhat reflect a similar philosophical tendency in the early XX century and in the thought of Vasconcelos himself: "The concept that underlies astrology, that the Cosmos constitutes a unity and that all parts of it are interdependent, is basic also to all the other pseudosciences. To make this principle effective in practice, it was necessary to know the laws of sympathy and antipathy by which the parts of the universe were related. But since these affinities could not be discovered by ordinary scientific methods, recourse was sought in divine revelation. There was a growing distrust of traditional Greek rationalism, and a breaking down of the distinction between science and religion. Hermes Thoth was but one, if perhaps the most important, of the gods and prophets (chiefly oriental) to whom men turned for divinely revealed wisdom". (*Britannica*, 1973, Vol. II, p. 434).

[20] Dravidian: Peoples of south and middle India where a Dravidian language is spoken. The term is purely linguistic since Dravidian-speaking peoples are of many different genetic types. Their origin and early history are obscure, and no specific racial element or prehistorical civilization can be associated with their first appearance in India. (*Britannica*, 1973, Vol. 7, p. 654). However, in general, Dravidians were dark skinned races that populated India previous to the Aryan invasion in the second millenium B.C. Intermarriage between Aryan tribesmen and dark-skinned Dravidians was one of the factors that produced the new Aryan-Indian culture. (See Trevor Ling, *History of Religion East and West*).

[21] By the Treaty of Tordesillas (1494) the world was divided between Spain and Portugal. Spain's rights of exploration were limited to lands more than 370 leagues west of the Cape Verde Islands (the Azores) and Portugal's to the east of this line. Thus Brazil, Africa, and the seaway to India were reserved for Portugal, the rest went to Spain. Pope Alexander VI (Rodrigo Borgia, 1431-1503), a Spaniard, as the vicar and representative of Christ on earth, was the arbiter, and ratified this treaty by a Papal Bull granting Spain and Portugal rights of exploration, conquest, and proselytizing of the lands thus divided.

[22] In 1588, the *Invincible Armada*, sent by the Spanish king, Phillip II, to attack England under the reign of Elizabeth I, was battered by a tempest off the English coast and defeated by the smaller and more maneuverable English fleet. This defeat marked the decline of Spanish, and the rise of English, sea power.

In 1805, the English fleet under Nelson defeated the French-Spanish fleets near the cape of Trafalgar, on the Spanish Atlantic coast. England's victory insured her power at sea and the security of her island against the European conquests by Napoleon.

Two years earlier, Napoleon had sold Louisiana to the United States, although he had sworn to the Spanish king never to cede this colony to any other power but Spain.

[23] Santiago de Cuba, Cavite, and Manila mark locations of Spanish defeats during the Spanish American War in 1898, both on the Cuban (Santiago) and the Asian (Cavite and Manila) fronts. As a result, Spain lost Cuba, Puerto Rico, and the Philippines, marking the end of the Spanish empire and the farthest extension of American imperial policy.

[24] In 1889, the *International Union of American Republics* was founded in Washington at the initiative of the United States. In 1910, the name was changed to *Pan American Union*, and in 1948, to its present name, *Organization of American States*.

[25] Father Miguel Hidalgo y Costilla (1753-1811). Mexican revolutionary hero. On the morning of September 15, 1810, he rallied a group of parishioners in front of his church in Dolores under the banner of the Virgin of Guadalupe, and to the cry of, ''Long live Independence! Long

live Our Lady of Guadalupe! Death to the Gachupines!'' (Grito de Dolores), initiated the fight for Mexican independence.

[26] Conspiración de Quito. Patriotic conspiration that proclaimed the independence of Ecuador from Spain on August 10, 1809.

[27] Simón Bolívar (1783-1830). Father of South American independence. Liberator of Venezuela, Colombia, Ecuador, Perú, and Bolivia, he tried to unite all of Latin America into a federation like the United States.

[28] Cuauhtémoc (1494?-1525). Nephew of Moctezuma and last Aztec emperor of Mexico, who resisted the siege of Tenochtitlán (Mexico City) by Hernán Cortés, but finally was captured and tortured by the Spaniards, who burned the soles of his feet, in order to learn the whereabouts of the royal treasure. Later he was executed by hanging, upon the order of Cortés.

[29] Atahualpa. Last *Inca* of Perú, was born at the beginning of the XVI century and died in 1533. It is said that Atahualpa, fascinated by Spanish knowledge of reading and writing, asked a soldier to write the name of God on his thumbnail. Afterwards, he would show his thumbnail to other officers and soldiers and all would pronounce the name. However, Pizarro, who did not know how to read, could not pronounce the word for the *Inca*. Atahualpa did not hide his contempt for Pizarro at this lack of ability, and this incident contributed to the decision to sentence Atahualpa to death.

[30] Hernán Cortés (1485-1547). Conqueror of Mexico.

[31] Francisco Pizarro (1475-1541). Conqueror of Peru.

[32] Pedro de Alvarado (1485?-1541). Companion of Cortés in the conquest of Mexico, and later conqueror of Guatemala, where he founded Santiago de los Caballeros de Guatemala (Guatemala City).

[33] Sebastián de Belalcázar (1495-1551). Conqueror of present day Ecuador, and founder of Quito and Guayaquil. The Barcelona edition reads ''Córdoba'' here, instead of Belalcázar.

91

[34] Diego Rodríguez de Silva y Velázquez (1599-1660). Royal painter to Phillip IV, a Hapsburg. Beginning in 1516, with the Emperor Charles V, this German royal family ruled Spain up to 1714. Some of Velázquez' most famous royal portraits in the Prado Museum include those of King Phillip IV, of Prince Baltasar Carlos on Horseback, of Queen Mariana of Austria, second wife to Phillip IV, and of the Infanta Margarita. The most famous painting of the royal household by Velázquez, "Las Meninas" (The Maids of Honor), is a portrait of the Infanta Margarita surrounded by maids of honour, dwarfs, dogs, Velázquez himself, and the king and queen in the background.

[35] Francisco José de Goya y Lucientes (1746-1828). Court painter to Charles III and to his son Charles IV, descendants of the French house of Bourbon, the ruling family in Spain from 1714 to the XX century. Goya's famous portrait of the royal household, "Family of Charles IV," in the Prado Museum is far from flattering, and depicts the ugliness and vulgarity of the principal figures so vividly as to produce the effect of caricature.

[36] Albion. Ancient Greek and Roman name for Britain. (From Celtic: *albain* — *alb, alp*, height, cliff, and *ban*, white).

[37] Buenos Aires was attacked in 1650, by the English pirate Thomas Cavendish, later knighted by Queen Elizabeth; Veracruz was looted in 1683; Havana was attacked without success by Sir Francis Drake, and suffered many other attacks by English, French and Dutch pirates; Campeche, in Yucatan, was plundered by English pirates in 1680; Panama was sacked and destroyed by Henry Morgan in 1671. These were but a few of the attacks suffered by Spanish colonies during the XVI and XVII centuries.

[38] Antonio José de Sucre (1795-1830). South American general, born in Venezuela, who fought with Bolívar for the Independence of Perú, Ecuador and Bolivia, and supported Bolívar's idea of a Latin American Union. This failed, though, and the continent became divided into smaller nations, like the Balkan Peninsula.

[39] Alejandro Sabes Petion (1770-1818). Father of Haitian Independence. Illegitimate son of a European colonist and a mulatto woman. His godmother gave him the nickname of *Petiot*, later corrupted to Petion, which he adopted as his family name.

[40] Francisco Xavier Mina (1789-1817). Spanish liberal and revolutionary who fought against Napoleon in Spain, and later in Mexico for the cause of the Mexican independence from Spain.

[41] Cortes of Cádiz. A parliamentary body convened by Spanish liberals in 1812, after the abdication of Ferdinand VII, the legitimate sovereign, in favor of Napoleon's brother, Joseph Bonaparte. The Cortes met in Cádiz to form a legitimate and Independent government for Spain, and to organize the fight against Napoleon. It proclaimed a liberal constitution, creating a parliamentary monarchy for Spain. Elsewhere in Spain, the people took arms against Napoleon and, with English help (Wellington), eventually succeeded in driving back the French. Events of this fight were immortalized in Goya's famous paintings, "El Dos de Mayo en Madrid," and "Fusilamientos del Dos de Mayo" (in the Prado Museum). This Napoleonic defeat in Spain, together with the retreat from the Russian front, marked the decline of Napoleonic power in Europe.

[42] Ferdinand VII (1784-1883). King of Spain during the Napoleonic invasion. Both he and his father, Charles IV, were forced by Napoleon to abdicate in favor of Napoleon's brother, Joseph Bonaparte. The Spaniards rejected the Napoleonic rule and fought the invadors in the so-called "War of Independence" to return Ferdinand VII to the throne. In the interim, most of Latin America declared independence from Spain. Ferdinand VII repaid his subjects by rejecting the liberal constitution proclaimed by the Cortes of Cádiz and by persecuting the liberals.

[43] José María Morelos y Pavón (1765-1815). Mexican Catholic priest who continued the fight for Mexican Independence from Spain initiated by Father Hidalgo who was executed in 1811.

[44] In 1816, Argentinian representatives met in Tucumán to officially declare independence from Spain and draft a new constitution (which, among other things, abolished slavery).

[45] During the latter part of the XIX century, the United States gradually reversed their previously liberal attitude towards immigration, partly due to economic and political reasons, but also to current theories of Anglo-Saxon racial superiority.

The U.S. Congress began the legal change by excluding further Chinese immigration in 1882. Exclusion of Japanese laborers was effected in 1908. Finally in 1921, and 1924, the United States adopted a frankly "racial" policy and established immigration quotas for different ethnic groups. Asian immigrants were excluded altogether. This system, with minor amendments áfter 1940 to allow Asian nationalities small quotas, survived until 1965 in spite of the discrediting of its racial theory in the 1930's and 1940's (*Americana*, 1972, Vol. 27, p. 501).

[46] "Cenote." Natural wells, typical of Yucatan, formed by subterranean rivers. These caverns and wells where the rivers came to the surface were used by the Maya Indians as sacred places for sacrifice or for bathing and watering. Their appearance is often striking since some of them occur as a sudden circular depression reaching great depths on an otherwise generally flat land.

[47] *Book of the Dead*. A collection of ancient Egyptian magical formulas preserved in papyrus scrolls buried with the dead, to guide them safely to the gates of the underworld. The *Book of the Dead* was known in the early Christian era and it has since been regarded within esoteric doctrine as symbolic instruction for the soul in her mystical journey.

[48] Three of the largest rivers in South America: The Amazon in Brazil, the Orinoco in Venezuela, and the Magdalena in Colombia.

[49] Cf. the essay "Nueva ley de los tres estados" in *Ideario de acción* (Lima: Ediciones Actual, 1924) págs. 51-64:

Esta ansia contemporánea de rebasar el patriotismo, de dilatar las fronteras, de celebrar pactos y alianzas según nuestro gusto y no de acuerdo con nuestras conveniencias materiales, este poderío del espíritu que en todos los órdenes se afirma avasallador nos permite formular una ley de desarrollo, una especie de "ley de los tres estados" — tomando de Comte sólo el nombre —, una ley de tres períodos de la organización de los pueblos.

El primero de estos estados es el período materialista en que el trato de tribu a tribu se sujeta a las necesidades y azares de las emigraciones y el trueque de los productos. La ley de este primer estado es la guerra.

El segundo período lo llamaremos intelectualista, porque durante él las relaciones internacionales se fundan en la conveniencia y el cálculo; comienza a triunfar la inteligencia sobre la fuerza bruta y se establecen fronteras estratégicas después de que la guerra ha definido el poder de cada nación. Los grandes imperios de la antigüedad participaron de los caracteres del primero y segundo períodos, y las nacionalidades modernas viven todavía en el segundo. El tercer período está por venir y lo llamaremos estético, porque en él las relaciones de los pueblos se regirán libremente por la simpatía y el gusto. El gusto que es ley suprema de la vida interior, y que hacia fuera se manifiesta como simpatía y belleza, llegará a ser entonces la norma indiscutible del orden público y de las relaciones entre los estados. (Also in *O.C.*, Vol. 2, p. 837).

[50] Comtian: From Auguste Comte (1798-1857), French philosopher, founder of Positivism, which he expounded in his *Cours de philosophie positive* (1830-1842). It divides the evolution of philosophical thought into three stages: Theological, metaphysical, and positivist. In the first stage, phenomena are explained as the result of the direct action of supernatural beings or forces. In the metaphysical stage, supernatural agents are replaced by abstract forces inherent in the nature of things. The last stage, the positivist (or scientific) renounces the search for absolute principles, and for the origin and destiny of the universe, and the final cause of phenomena, limiting itself to discover, by the use of reason and observation, the relations of cause and effect that regulate phenomena, that is, the laws of nature.

[51] Mendel's laws. The basic principles of heredity, discovered by Austrian biologist Gregor Mendel (1822-1884), tracing the regular patterns of the separation and distribution of genetic characteristics in hybrids.

[52] From Greek *palin*, again, and *genesis*, birth.

[53] Jakob Johann Baron von Uexküll (1864-1945). German biologist or physiologist born in Estonia. His main work was the study of the physiology of the nerves and muscles of invertebrate animals. His research led him to stress the autonomy of the nervous muscular units of the lower

animals, describing the sea urchin as a "republic of reflexes". He later came to the conclusion that it was necessary to postulate some higher, non-material, coordinating influence, an idea developed in his *Theoretische Biologie* (1920). His position thus falls within the philosophical view of Vitalism, that a special life-principle or essence distinguishes living from non-living matter. This life-principle directs living matter to perfect itself, providing the basis of evolution. For a recent statement of this position, see Albert Szent-Gyoirgi, "Drive in living matter to perfect itself" (in *Synthesis*, Spring, 1974, Vol 1, no. 1, pp. 12-24). The complexity and synchronism of molecular changes necessary for biological modifications is so tremendous, that random mutation must be considered insufficient as a cause of evolution.

[54] Although no specific reference was provided by Vasconcelos for the quotation in his text, see Uexküll, *Theoretical Biology*, New York: Harcourt, Brace and Co., 1926):

The finished cell is not an independent structure, but, as soon as it has reached complete development, it is connected, conformably with plan, not only to its neighbors but to all the cells of the body. This result could be achieved only if initiation of the various part-processes during genesis went on in perfect accordance with plan; and this again presupposes a hidden framework in the ferments that give the impetus (p. 194).

[55] No specific reference provided by Vasconcelos, however for a discussion of the significance of Mendel's discoveries according to Uexküll, see Chapter VI, "The Genesis of Living Organisms," *op. cit.*, pp. 178-235.

[56] Plato's dialogue (between Socrates and Phaedrus) on the subject of beauty; an exhortation to the love of perfect beauty.

[57] Perhaps Vasconcelos was following in this design an old Egyptian tradition. Compare the following footnote in Edouard Schuré, *The Ancient Mysteries of the East*, (New York: Multimedia Publishing Corp. 1973), p. 127:

This division of mankind into four successive, primitive races was accepted by the oldest priests of Egypt. They are represented by four figures of different types and skin colors in the paintings of the tomb of Seti I at Thebes. The red race bears the name *Rot*; the Asiatic race with yellow skin, *Amu*; the African race with black skin, *Halasiu*; the Lybico European race with white skin and blond hair, *Tamahu* — Lenormant, *History of the Peoples of the Orient*, Vol. I.

Afterword to the 1997 Edition
by Joseba Gabilondo

José Vasconcelos wrote *La Raza Cósmica* in 1925,[1] at a moment when Mexico, after the 1910 Revolution and at the beginning of the decline of the neocolonial order, set out to become a modern nation-state —a project whose results were to be evaluated twenty-five years later by another Mexican intellectual, Octavio Paz, in *The Labyrinth of Solitude*, his *compte rendue* essay on the project of Mexican modernity.[2]

In *La raza cósmica* race is the central articulation, one that is simultaneously mythic, historical, present, and utopian. No modern European discourse could take such an approach in 1925.[3] In this respect Vasconcelos's work is not modern. By raising the problem of race, his work opened up a Latin American position from which to confront modernity's main political and cultural materialization, the nation-state. Thus, Vasconcelos confronted the modern institution of the nation-state and the formation of its historical hegemony, positing race as the historical formation that exceeds both the nation-state and modernity.

Vasconcelos's work is important today precisely because the new Latin American theories on postmodernity arise just as Latin America is debating the need to abandon the modern project of the nation-state and renegotiate its place in the new postmodern history.[4] At this moment, Vasconcelos's discourse on race recovers a new urgency as the work that attempted to negotiate a position in relation to modernity and its institutions, not unconditionally but critically. It seems that the contemporary Latin American exit from modernity, or its abandonment, needs to be approached in the same critical manner; otherwise there is a risk of a blind embrace of postmodernity, which is bound to duplicate the mistakes made when modernity was entered.

In this context of re-evaluating modernity and the nation-state, Vasconcelos's mobilization of race needs to be re-examined; it is utterly different from most racial theorizations of its time, such as that of José Carlos Mariátegui (1895-1930).[5] Mariátegui resorts to class as the primary axis of history, which encompasses race and thereby resituates it within the confines of the nation-state. Similar attempts by critics such

99

as Paul Gilroy to reread earlier modern authors' work in relation to post-modernity have become essential to rethinking the postmodern scenario of the "after the nation-state" moment, particularly in relation to Black subjectivity and Black studies. In Gilroy's words:

> Though largely ignored by recent debates over modernity and its discontents, these ideas about nationality, ethnicity, authenticity, and cultural integrity are characteristically modern phenomena that have profound implications for cultural criticism and cultural history. . . . Any shift towards a postmodern condition should not, however, mean that the conspicuous power of these modern subjectivities and the movements they articulated has been left behind. Their power has, if anything, grown, and their ubiquity as a means to make political sense of the world is currently unparalleled by the languages of class and socialism by which they once appeared to have been surpassed.[6]

In this context, Vasconcelos's work on race suddenly becomes a necessary site to revisit in order to effect a successful political and cultural articulation of postmodernity in Latin America and elsewhere. As George Yúdice notes in his evaluation of postmodernity and transnational capitalism in Latin America, tradition can be recycled in new political and cultural practices without having to resuscitate it as modern—that is, as belonging to the nation-state structure: "The criteria, forms, and terms of these [postmodern] rearticulatory practices are both old and new: old because they draw from their traditions; new because they no longer operate solely within the framework of class or nation."[7] It is not a coincidence that Chicano and Chicana writers have been the first to reuse Vasconcelos's work in new and original ways. These writers articulate their position from an awareness of not belonging to the formation of the nation-state; they come after modernity.[8]

José Vasconcelos (1881-1959) occupied several positions within the educational apparatus of postrevolutionary Mexico, serving first as secretary of education, and then as president of the National University between 1914 and 1924. After his political rival Plutarco Elías Calles took the presidency in 1924, Vasconcelos traveled throughout Europe and the United States and wrote his two best-known works: *La raza cósmica*

(*The Cosmic Race*, 1925) and *Indología* (*Indology*, 1929). He returned to Mexico in 1927 and, in 1929, ran for office as a presidential candidate. After his defeat, he consecrated the rest of his life to a prolific production of mostly philosophical and autobiographical writings. Later still, he moved to conservative and fundamentalist positions.[9] Vasconcelos is credited with having developed a successful democratization of the educational system in Mexico. The institutional development of the famous Mexican muralist school of painters (Rivera and Orozco, among others) is one of his finest achievements.[10]

Vasconcelos belongs to a new generation of Latin American and Spanish writers that began to be known under the new label, just then inaugurated, of "intellectuals"—writers who were invested in the production of speculative discourses which had traditionally been grouped under the genre of the essay and centered on the issue of the nation. As Doris Sommer argues, earlier generations of Latin American writers cultivated the novel, and more specifically the romance, as a way to deal with the problem of national construction. Sommer explains the function and specificity of this novelistic production: "to marry national destiny to personal sentimentalism was precisely what made these books peculiarly American." The final goal of these narratives was "to produce legitimate citizens, literally to engender civilization."[11]

At the turn of the century, Vasconcelos's generation shifted its interest to the production of essays, which reflected a desire to be legitimized as a distinct class of intellectuals and educators in charge of such discourse. This phenomenon, which had been widespread in Europe, at least since the Dreyfuss affair in France (1898), was concerned with the naturalization of the nation as the site of discursive production. The intellectual became the producer of national discourse in the form of a problem, polemic, or question, which in turn became "the" national problem with universal dimensions. The Generation of 1898 in Spain and its search for a Spanish identity through the debate of *casticismo* paralleled some of the later Latin American debates.[12]

Within the Latin American context, Vasconcelos belongs to the young generation of intellectuals that included the Mexicans Antonio Caso (1883-1946) and Alfonso Reyes (1889-1959),[13] the Peruvian José Carlos Mariátegui (1895-1930), and the Dominican Pedro Henríquez Ureña (1884-1946), a group that criticized the imperialist consequences of modernity and its turn-of-the-century ideology of positivism.[14] They were influenced by the first two Latin American writers elaborating a postpositivist thought about imperialism and modernity: the Cuban José Martí (1853-1895) and the Uruguayan José Enrique Rodó (1871-1917).[15] As Vasconcelos's generation would prove, the production of a national discourse became inseparable from the problem of modernity and imperialism in Latin America.

Martí was the first to perceive the conflict that Latin America was to face with modernity as a result of the shift of hegemony to the North. However, as his most famous article, "Our America" (1891), shows, Martí is unable to imagine a critical position in regard to modernity: he continuously aligns Latin America with nature. In the article, Martí responds to the positivist philosophy of the previous generation, which attempted to impose modernity in Latin America by erasing native history. More precisely, Martí paraphrases the well-known positivist slogan consecrated by Argentinean president Domingo Faustino Sarmiento (1811-1888), "Civilization or Barbarism," in order to elaborate his own position vis-à-vis modernity: "The struggle is not between barbarity and civilization, but between false erudition and nature. The natural man is good."[16]

Later on in the article, as he attempts to formulate the agency of the Latin American subject and its specificity, Martí again locates political agency in nature: "The natural people, driven by instinct, swept away the golden staffs of office in blind triumph. The European or Yankee book could not provide the answer to the Hispanic-American enigma."[17] This naturalizing of politics lies in the need to save a universal subject position that is critical of modernity. In other words, Martí attempts to find a place for the universality promised by modernity, but denied by the imperialist order, to any colonial subject. This contradictory space is found by Martí in nature. Accordingly, this assertion of nature forces Martí to obliterate the political implications of race in Latin America. For Martí, race, in any of its formulations, would deny the possibility of a modern and universal place in nature; race would imply difference within nature and thus a lack of universality. Resorting to the pre-nineteenth century formulation of race as lineage, a nonbiological category equivalent to the more modern one of civilization,[18] Martí argues that "there can be no racial hate, because there are no races. The rachitic thinkers and theorists juggle and warm over the library-shelf races, which the open-minded traveler and well-disposed observer seek in vain in *Nature*'s justice, where the *universal identity of man* leaps forth from triumphant love and the turbulent lust for life."[19] Martí wants to present race as an old-fashioned academic issue, left behind by modernity.

102

When Rodó published *Ariel* in 1900, the United States was engaged in the annexation of Puerto Rico and the Philippines, which also brought to a symbolic end the Hispanic imperial prepotence of the past. In this context, Rodó begins his speculation by marking the difference between both Americas, Latin America and the United States, and does so by referring to race. In this context "race" still means the older idea of "civilization." By introducing race in this way, Rodó abandons Martí's attempt to situate modernity in nature and proceeds to reposition modernity across "the two American races" he elaborates, even if to do so amounts to abandoning Martí's universalism. Rodó, then, is the first intellectual to utilize race to frame the new geopolitical organization of the Americas already advanced by Martí. Rodó's new mobilization of race is the one that Vasconcelos will take up.

Starting off from the "racial" divide between the two Americas, Rodó still attempts to salvage modernity for Latin America by claiming that the duality characterizing modernity is embodied in the two racially differentiated Americas. Through the allegorical use of Shakespeare's two characters in *The Tempest,* Ariel and Caliban, Rodó borrows terminology from antimodernist discourses to characterize the United States as negativity—and thus redefine, by default, Latin America as its positive complement. The United States becomes the site of all modern negativity: cosmopolitanism, alienation, reification, amassment, degeneration, history, etc. Accordingly, Latin America reclaims modernity's positivity: tradition, humanity, utopia, genius, etc. As Rodó repeatedly claims:

> We Latin-Americans have an inheritance of Race, a great ethnic tradition to maintain, a sacred bond which unites us to immortal pages of history and puts us on our honour to preserve this for the future. That cosmopolitanism which we have to respect as the irresistible tendency of our development need not exclude that sentiment of fidelity to the past, nor that moulding and directing force of which the genius of our race must avail itself in the fusing of the elements that shall constitute the American of the future.[20]

In Rodó's hierarchical reversion, North America still remains the necessary and constitutive negativity of modernity; hence Rodó's reference to *America*, in the singular, as modernity's utopian horizon. He believes that there will be a future America, differentiated by its two races, which will reincarnate modernity. Race, for Rodó, still does not have the imperialist implications that it will develop later, as a result of the appropriation of biological theories for the legitimization of white supremacy.[21] As Rodó argues, "if one can dimly foresee even a higher concord in the future, that will be due not to a one-sided imitation of one race by the other, but to a reciprocity of influences and a skilful [sic] harmonizing of those attributes which make the peculiar glory of either race [la gloria de las dos]."[22]

Only in the twentieth century, after the various North American interventions in Latin America and the Mexican revolution, will modernity, for the first time, no longer be perceived by Vasconcelos's generation as coextensive with America. Furthermore, Latin American governments will attempt to rechannel the idea of modernity through the construction of national cultures in their respective states, making the project of modernity coincide with that of the nation-state. At this threshold, Vasconcelos reclaims the importance of race in a new sense, which I will discuss, in order to renegotiate modernity. However, his discourse no longer attempts to articulate a space within the project of modernity already embodied by North American imperialism, but rather a space situated in relation to modernity—a space that will no longer be American but Latin American.[23]

The double position occupied by Vasconcelos as both an intellectual and a political figure in the construction of the Mexican nation-state made him aware of the importance of race in the historicity of both Latin America and its forming nation-states. This awareness of the specific historical interface between Latin America and its nation-states is what differentiates Vasconcelos's work from that of most of his contemporaries and makes it, after Rodó's, the most influential of its time among the new Latin American youth. But some of his contemporaries present a better intellectual formation, or a more solid intellectual or political position. Mariátegui, for example, develops a much more sophisticated and comprehensive Marxist study of Peru, but his Marxist discourse is always historically confined by the Peruvian state, to the point that it becomes the discourse's natural framework of reference.[24] Similarly, the more philosophical work developed by Antonio Caso shows a better formation and a more elaborate philosophical discourse, but nevertheless remains confined to the Mexican state and its cultural project.[25] Octavio Paz captures Vasconcelos's historical importance:

104

This Ibero-American philosophy [of Vasconcelos] was the first attempt to resolve the conflict that had been latent in the Revolution from the beginning. . . . Vasconcelos tried to resolve the question by offering his philosophy of the Ibero-American race. The motto of positivism, "Love, Order and Progress," was replaced by a proud boast: "The Spirit Shall Speak through My Race."[26]

Only Vasconcelos understood that the historical interface between Latin America and its nation-states is the position from which modernity can be faced. As his repeated antinationalist statements show ("Our emancipators rang the sounds of Balkan glories"),[27] he was well aware of the risks involved in reducing the project of modernity solely to the institution of the nation-state. However—and as the genealogy of Martí and Rodó proves—he was also aware that Latin America, because of its new geopolitical position as the area of imperialist expansion of the United States, is no longer the repository of modernity. In a passage referring to his stay in Chile he illustrates his historical position:

When talking to me, several people asked the same question: If I had declared myself in favor of internationalism in the speech I gave the evening before, why then had my work in the Public Education of Mexico been nationalist? We need to stimulate our national culture, I replied, because we have in front of us a culture that is powerful and imperialist [the United States]. However, in order to strengthen our national culture, it is necessary that our nationalism becomes continental and *lies its foundations not only on political but also ethnic grounds*. In this wider sense, it is necessary for us to remain nationalist until we are able to achieve a true internationalism, that is, as soon as the dangers of the many imperialisms that attempt to subjugate, not to civilize, disappear.[28]

In order to articulate his position, Vasconcelos deploys a very specific formulation of race, which opens up a historical space with potential and multiple political and cultural possibilities that neither a nationalist nor a continentalist position could capture separately: "If our patriotism does not identify with the many phases of the old conflict between Latinos and Anglo-Saxons, we will never succeed in making it overcome the traits of a regionalism without universal spirit. . . . In order to never give up the motherland [*patria*] itself, it is necessary that we live up to the high importance of race.[29]

Vasconcelos, unlike his predecessors, mobilizes a more contemporary reformulation of race that nevertheless remains nonmodern. He states that race is the discourse by which imperialism is expanding as the global phenomenon that addresses the colonial world as racially marked.[30] Hence, Vasconcelos's urgency to think race. However, he simultaneously deploys different historical theories of race, which are incompatible from a modern point of view, in order to build a racial theory that will confront modernity. Vasconcelos articulates race as lineage or civilization, as biological type, and as the interface of imperial globalization. By deploying all these racial theories simultaneously, he opens a space for Latin America which is (1) specific both culturally and biologically, (2) global because it participates in the racial interface of imperialism, and (3) utopian because it situates Latin America in the center of the future outcome of modernity's present racial contradictions. This *bricolage* of racial theories effected by Vasconcelos is what allows him to produce a discourse that exceeds modernity and reopens a historical space for Latin America that is critical of modernity. I call this discourse "utopian realism."[31]

As I discussed above, Martí and Rodó still had recourse to the pre-nineteenth-century articulation of race as lineage or civilization. In turn, Vasconcelos rescued the nineteenth-century idea of race as a biological type, but without renouncing the older sense of race as lineage. The newer articulation of race as biological type was developed by Georges Cuvier in France and Samuel George Morton in the United States, respectively, and remained prevalent until the Darwinist revolution. This articulation was the first to establish correspondences between biological and cultural types. These racial theories also gave rise to the naturalization of geopolitical hegemonies inaugurated by European colonialism and consolidated by North American imperialism.[32] In Vasconcelos's case, his double deployment of race as both lineage and biological type serves, first of all, to redefine the Latin American continent as a space biologically and culturally separate from modernity.[33] At the same time, Vasconcelos also addresses the newest theories on race derived from Darwin's and Mendel's doctrines on evolution. By doing so, he challenges imperialism's globalization and, by further elaborating on

106

the contradictions of these racial theories, he opens a utopian sp
Latin America.

Following the revision of creationist theories spurred by Darwi
evolutionism, Vasconcelos first reworks a new mythical version of
polygenetic evolution of races. His polygenetic theory accounts for t
Latin American specificity not only of a natural position but also of .
natural genealogy. Similar to Joseph Arthur Gobineau in his theory on
the Aryan race and its decadence,[34] Vasconcelos, using Wegener's theory
on the formation of continents, posits Atlantis as the origin of the "red"
race (native Americans), whose degeneration left as its only traces the
Aztec and Inca cultures in Latin America. His racial genealogy is completed with references to the Spaniards' invasion of Latin America, the
introduction of slavery, and the resulting hybridization of the "red,
black, and white" races.

Although Vasconcelos accepts the anticreationist implications of Darwinian evolutionism, he refuses to incorporate the Darwinian theory of
the selection of species, as developed by Herbert Spencer, into his articulation of race. He understood that such application would only legit-
imize the British and North American imperialist hegemony as the result
of the natural selection of races. Thus, he uses the globalizing implications of the Darwinian theory of evolution without invoking its imperialist repercussions:

> The British preach natural selection, with the tacit conse-
> quence that the kingdom of this world belongs, by natural
> and divine law, to the dolichocephalous of the islands and its
> descendants. But one must fight this science that succeeds
> in invading us with the crafts of the conquering trade, as one
> fights any imperialism: placing a superior science and a
> wider and more vigorous civilization in front of it.[35]

Later on, in order to counteract the social implications of the Darwinian theory of selection, Vasconcelos applies Mendel's theories of reproduction to his mythic account of a Latin American race. This combination yields a new theory of racial history in modernity. Vasconcelos
posits that only the *hybridization* of the four races that constitute, according to him, the human species (red, yellow, black, and white), will
yield the utopian human being predicated by modernity. By combining
the most modern effect of imperialist racism triggered by Darwinism—

...del's theories of reproduction and hybridiza-
...odern utopia in which racial hybridization,
...supremacy, is the only possible answer.
...ation is explained by Vasconcelos as happening
...humankind's history: in the future, selection will
...e according to the physical constraints imposed by
...ive, but rather by "aesthetic affinity." By aestheticizing
...Vasconcelos reintroduces selection without its imperialist
...ons, in a posteugenic fashion, as it were.[36]
...ly, Vasconcelos proceeds to claim that Latin America was the
...ent *topos* in which the formation of such a racially hybrid utopia
...was already taking place. In other words, because Latin America was
the only continent in which the "black, red, yellow, and white" races had
already mixed, Vasconcelos claims that Latin America was meant to be
the utopian *topos* that will give rise to the fifth, or cosmic, race. This
utopian race, because of its hybridity, would bring humankind to a new
stage of development, beyond modernity.[37]

Through the *bricolage* of different racial theories, Vasconcelos's discourse expands from cosmogony to cosmology: from Atlantis and the
"red" race to the cosmic race of modernity's utopia. At a time when no
new post-Darwinian racial theories were emerging but when the heyday
of white supremacist theories still lingered,[38] Vasconcelos posits a new
kind of discourse that, in its modernity, exceeds the epistemological limits of any human science of its time. In this way, *La raza cósmica* steps
into what we would now consider "fiction" or "literature" in its strong
sense. At the expense of being considered a "fictional or imperfect account," by this shift, Vasconcelos opens up a new discursive space which
contains modernity.[39]

This metamodern, or megamodern, moment, effected by Vasconcelos's formulation of race, opens up a historical space for Latin America
from which modernity can be politically negotiated. This form of excessive modernity, characteristic of Vasconcelos, could be named "mythic
realism" or "utopian realism." In either case, it is genealogically related
to other forms of Latin American discourse that clash with modernity:
pre-Columbian discourses, travel and testimony narratives, and magic
realism. From Vasconcelos's work, one can see that the dystopian effect
that the later literature of magic realism had is related to the enclosure of
the Latin American experience within the confines of the nation-state.[40]

Unfortunately, the utopian realism prevailing in the prologue of *La raza cósmica* is followed by a more traditional narrative of Vasconcelos's voyages to Brazil, Uruguay, Argentina, and Chile. The tension between these two different discourses—utopian prologue and travel narrative—unveils the limits and tensions of the book. Vasconcelos traveled through those countries as a diplomat of the Mexican government, a representative of the Mexican nation-state, a specifically national subject. Consequently, he encountered other authorities and diplomats who represented their own respective nationalities. As a result, his travel narrative was made possible by the institution of the nation-state and thus only narrates his encounters with other representations of the nation-state. The two main objects Vasconcelos describes in his travel narratives are politicians and nature.

One could argue that the historical reality opened by race in the prologue of the book is canceled in the following travel narrative by the epistemological myopia generated by Vasconcelos's political position as national representative. Furthermore, the only productive instances of meaning are derived from comparisons between nation-states. This is best illustrated by Vasconcelos's narration about an encounter with some Chilean students in opposition to the government:

> I took advantage of my exposition of the Mexican revolution to proceed to depict identical situations I believed existed in Chile. Soon I realized I was able to unveil parallels, for every time I finished the account of some Mexican misery, the boys shouted: "The same here. The same here." As I saw that my plan was working thanks to the public's cooperation, all I had to do was to denounce the injustices of Mexican situations of different periods; the boys did the rest.[41]

In other words, once utopian realism loses its excessive modernity and becomes a punctual narrative in a given historical time, the nation-state reappears as the only reality and, conversely, the history and politics enacted by race become marginal. Vasconcelos's "I" becomes the new discursive subject, a subject that, as Sylvia Molloy convincingly argues, was meant to collapse with the nation-state and become the latter's subject: a national subject, very much in line with the genealogy of megalomaniac leaders and dictators of Latin America.[42] These are some of the contradictions that close *La raza cósmica*.

As Lourdes Martínez Echazábal rightly points out, once the racial discourse of Vasconcelos was retaken by national governments and intellectuals in the 1930s, it became a liberal version of "racial harmony" upheld by the hegemonic classes to "strengthen the national self-consciousness" that legitimizes them ideologically.[43] Later racial theories, such as Gilberto Freyre's (Brazil) and Fernando Ortiz's (Cuba), have suffered similar liberal appropriations. Octavio Paz hints at the reason behind the liberal neutralization of Vasconcelos's theories: "Unfortunately his philosophy was a personal creation, the very opposite of that of the liberals and positivists, who had been part of a vast ideological current. . . . It is an isolated monument and has not originated any schools or movements."[44]

At this time, as Latin America and the world exit modernity and abandon one of its most important political institutions, the nation-state, Vasconcelos's *La raza cósmica* can be reread as the discourse that reminds us of the importance of race in dealing with this historical moment.[45] Furthermore, if *La raza cósmica* is read backwards—from the punctual time of Vasconcelos's travel narrative to the opening utopian realism of the prologue—the real contemporary meaning of *La raza cósmica* can be unfolded: the passage from the nation-state to race. Vasconcelos's influence in formulating the Chicano celebration of "La raza" cannot be explained otherwise: his influence is most meaningful to those who do not fall within the limits of the nation-state.

When theories of hybridization are heralded by contemporary postmodern theorists in the Americas and elsewhere, as in the case of Néstor García Canclini and Homi Bhabha,[46] Vasconcelos's work reminds us that race exceeds modernity's institutions while constituting them. More than ever before, race is one of the sites, beyond scientific or political reification, at which the historical moment of contemporary globalization and capitalism can be politically grasped.[47]

The present edition of *La raza cósmica* is reprinted from the bilingual version edited by Didier T. Jaén in 1979, with the sponsorship of the Department of Chicano Studies at UCLA for the *Pensamiento Mexicano* series of the *Centro de Publicaciones*. Jaén's edition contains only the original prologue of *La raza cósmica*. The other chapters that narrate Vasconcelos's travels throughout Latin America were eliminated in his edition, which is sensible given the fact that *La raza cósmica's* historical influence is due to its prologue. The travel narratives that follow in the original offer no information, beyond the anecdotal, that alters the historical reception and influence of *La raza cósmica*.

This 1997 edition also maintains the critical introduction written by Jaén for the 1979 edition. The more humanist and spiritualist approach of his introduction reflects some of the concerns of the Chicano reappropriation of Vasconcelos's work during the late 1970s. Jaén's statement that "Vasconcelos' essay on the Cosmic race, then, is not simply a racist [=racial] theory, but a theory of the future development of human consciousness,"[48] encapsulates the historical and political context of such reappropriation. Since Vasconcelos's work cannot be read apart from its ulterior historical readings and reappropriations, Jaén's introduction is important as a historical document accounting for some of the many layers of "meaning" Vasconcelos's work has accumulated since its original publication. Finally, the inclusion of the new prologue written by Vasconcelos for the second edition of *La raza cósmica* in 1948, as well as an introduction that contains a detailed biography, an extensive apparatus of notes and a bibliography, make Jaén's edition unparalleled. The current afterword is meant to complement Jaén's introduction with an expanded bibliography and an update on the discussions that have taken place since 1979.

Jaén's translation faithfully maintains most of the formality and rigidity of the intellectual Spanish style current in Vasconcelos's time. Only the long, baroque cadence of Vasconcelos's prose has sometimes been broken in the translation into several shorter English sentences. Such a version might not capture the historical specificity and literalness of Vasconcelos's style to the last detail, thus going against certain translation traditions that would still like to uphold uncompromising literalism as the way to attain "truthfulness." Jaén's version perhaps better captures the historical and political meaning that Vasconcelos's work has regained after its Chicano reappropriation. In this respect, the English reader cannot hope for a translation more faithful to the history of *La raza cósmica* than Jaén's.

Notes

I want to thank José Muñoz, Juan G. Gelpí, Celestia Ward, and Gary Pratt for their help in writing this afterword.

[1] José Vasconcelos, *La raza cósmica: misión de la raza iberoamericana; notas de viajes a la América del Sur* (N.p.: Agencia Mundial de Librería, n.d.). *La raza cósmica* was included in the second volume of Vasconcelos's complete works: *Obras Completas,* 4 vols. (Mexico City: Libreros Mexicanos Unidos, 1957-1961), 903-1067. All quotations in English from *La raza cósmica* are my own translation. For a comprehensive bibliography, see David William Foster, "A Checklist of Criticism on José Vasconcelos," *Los Ensayistas* 14-15 (March 1983): 177-212.

[2] Octavio Paz, *The Labyrinth of Solitude, the Other Mexico, and Return to the Labyrinth of Solitude, Mexico and the United States and The Philanthropic Ogre* (New York: Grove Press, 1985).

[3] Obviously, the connection of Vasconcelos's work with the European avant-garde and its manifestos (from futurism to surrealism) is clear. However, no avant-garde manifesto steps out of the aesthetic realm, even when invoking politics.

Sánchez-Macgregor, on the other hand, emphasizes the final aesthetic unity of Vasconcelos's work, approximating it to the avant-garde, although teleologically. See Joaquin Sánchez-Macgregor, "La estética de Vasconcelos como proyecto utópico," *Cuadernos americanos* 6.1/31 (January-February 1992): 246-51.

[4] See George Yúdice, Jean Franco, and Juan Flores, eds., *On Edge: The Crisis of Contemporary Latin American Culture* (Minneapolis: University of Minnesota Press, 1992); John Beverly, "The Politics of Latin American Postmodernism," *Against Literature* (Minneapolis: University of Minnesota Press, 1993), 103-23; Néstor García-Canclini, *Culturas híbridas. Estrategias para entrar y salir de la modernidad* (Mexico City: Grijalbo, 1989); Christopher Mitchell, ed., *Changing Perspectives in Latin American Studies: Insights from Six Disciplines* (Stanford: Standford University Press, 1988).

[5] José Carlos Mariátegui, *Seven Interpretive Essays on Peruvian Reality* (Austin: University of Texas Press, 1971).

112

[6] Paul Gilroy, *The Black Atlantic: Modernity and Double Consciousness* (Cambridge: Harvard University Press, 1993), 2. One must add language to the list of modern phenomena Gilroy gives. From a Latin or Hispanic perspective, it is clear that Gilroy's anglophone construction of the black Atlantic, because of its linguistic reification of black race as anglophone, obliterates the black Hispanic and Brazilian participation, among others. Such obliteration runs against his own argument.

[7] George Yúdice, "Postmodernity and Transnational Capitalism in Latin America," in Yúdice, et al., *On Edge* 23-24.

[8] For examples of very different Chicano recuperations of Vasconcelos's work, see Gloria Anzaldúa, *Borderlands/La Frontera: The New Mestiza* (San Francisco: Aunt Lute Books, 1987), 77, and Andrés G. Guerrero, "The Secular-Religious Symbol of *La Raza Cósmica,*" *A Chicano Theology* (New York: Orbis Books, 1987), 118-37.

[9] In the new prologue Vasconcelos wrote in 1948 for the second edition of *La raza cósmica,* he clearly turned to more conservative positions and embraced a more traditional version of the "old Catholic doctrine." His new conservative position, however, did not alter his views on the cosmic race and hybridization. This second prologue has been included in this edition (see pp. 2-5).

[10] For a complete account of Vasconcelos's life see Alfonso Taracena, *José Vasconcelos (*Mexico City: Editorial Porrúa, 1982); Itzhak Bar-Lewaw Mulstock, *José Vasconcelos; vida y obra* (Mexico City: Clásica Selecta Editora Librera, 1965); Gabriella De Beer, *José Vasconcelos and His World* (New York: Las Américas, 1966); and José Joaquín Blanco, *Se llamaba Vasconcelos. Una evocación crítica* (Mexico City: Fondo de Cultura Económica, 1977).

[11] Doris Sommer, "Irresistible Romance: the Foundational Fictions of Latin America," *Nation and Narration,* ed. Homi K. Bhabha (New York: Routledge, 1990), 84, 86.

[12] See E. Inman Fox, "El 98 y el origen de los 'intelectuales,'" *La crisis intelectual del 98* (Madrid: Cuadernos para el Diálogo, 1976), 9-16; see also Julio Ramos, *Desencuentros de la modernidad en América*

Latina: Literatura y política en el siglo XIX (Mexico City: Fondo de Cultura Económica, 1989).

[13] I refer to all the intellectuals as a single historical generation, which runs contrary to the general trend of considering only the Mexican intellectuals as a "generation." The name given to them is *los contemporaneos* or *Generación del Ateneo*. See Guillermo Sheridan, *Los contemporaneos* (Mexico City: Fondo de Cultura Económica, 1985).

[14] For a more detailed account of Latin American positivism and racism, see Lourdes Martínez-Echazábal, "Positivismo y Racismo en el Ensayo Hispanoamericano," *Cuadernos Americanos* 2.3 (1988): 121-29.

[15] For an assessment of this generation and an account of its antipositivist reaction, see the excellent anthology edited by Leopoldo Zea, *Precursores del pensamiento latinoamericano contemporaneo* (Mexico City: SepTentas, 1971). For a more detailed and disciplinary account within the philosophical institution, especially in reference to the relation between Vasconcelos and Antonio Caso, see Jorge J. E. Gracia, ed., *Latin American Philosophy in the Twentieth Century* (Buffalo: Prometheus Books, 1986), 27-31.
Needless to say, besides Martí and Rodó, the European antipositivist reaction of idealists and vitalists such as Nietzsche and Bergson provided the philosophical basis for Vasconcelos's generation.

[16] José Martí, "Our America," *The América of José Martí,* ed. and trans. Juan de Onís (New York: Noonday Press, 1953), 141-42.

[17] Ibid. 147.

[18] Michael Banton, *Racial Theories* (Cambridge: Cambridge University Press, 1987), 1-27.

[19] Martí, "Our America," 150; my emphasis.

[20] José Rodó, *Ariel,* trans. F. J. Stimson (Cambridge: Riverside Press, 1922), 93-94.

[21] Banton, *Racial Theories,* 29-64.

[22] Rodó, *Ariel*, 95.

[23] Rick Langhorst, "Los Estados Unidos vistos por José Vasconcelos," *Los Ensayistas* 10-11 (March 1981): 117-22.

[24] Mariátegui, *Seven Interpretive Essays.*

[25] Tomás Mallo, "El antipositivismo en Mexico," *Cuadernos Hispanoamericanos* (December 1982): 624-37. Mallo traces the history of the introduction of the concept of race by Justo Sierra as well as the influence of European idealism and vitalism (in the works of Kant, Nietzsche, Bergson, etc.) on such racial elaboration.

[26] Paz, *Labyrinth*, 154-55.

[27] Vasconcelos, *La raza cósmica*, 11.

[28] Ibid., 268; my emphasis.

[29] Ibid., 7.

[30] Eric Hobsbawn, *Age of Empire (1875-1914)* (New York: Vintage Books, 1989).

[31] Vasconcelos also refers to this double bind by the term *objetivismo idealista;* see Sánchez-Macgregor, "La estética," 247.

[32] Banton, *Racial Theories,* 72-79.

[33] Spain and Puerto Rico also become nations in which similar ideas of race/ethnicity developed. In both countries, curiously enough, racial discourses are the basis on which a dystopian national identity is elaborated in terms of antimodernism and death (see Unamuno) or disease (see Zeno Gandía). For Spain, see Manuel de Unamuno *En torno al casticismo* (1895). For Puerto Rico and Zeno Gandía, see the critical work of Juan G. Gelpí, *Literatura y paternalismo en Puerto Rico* (San Juan, P.R.: Editorial de la Universidad de Puerto Rico, 1993).

[34] Gobineau also "explained" the origin of a "Mexican" and "Peruvian" civilization; see Banton, *Racial Theories,* 47.

[35] Vasconcelos, *La raza cósmica,* 33. Vasconcelos's attacks on social Darwinism respond to what Donna Haraway calls "situated knowledge" and "strong science." See Donna J. Haraway, *Simians, Cyborgs, and Women: The Reinvention of Nature* (New York: Routledge, 1991).

[36] This is the "sublime moment of race" according to Vasconcelos, in which race loses its "purposefulness" and becomes purely aesthetic. However, beyond the merit of the attempt itself, I have serious reservations as to whether Vasconcelos's racial aesthetization would not lead to some form of fascist, aesthetic eugenics. Peter Earl hints at this possibility when he refers to the later fascist sympathies Vasconcelos developed. See Peter Earl, "Utopía, Universópolis, Macondo," *Hispanic Review* 50.2 (1982), 148-49.

In a final analysis, I would rather propose that, historically, Vasconcelos's aesthetic move was the only tactically possible response to social Darwinism. His later sympathies toward fascism would have to be explained as an extreme reaction against Mexican nationalism rather than as a forthright embrace of fascism.

[37] Although there is no room here for an orientalist analysis of Vasconcelos's work, it is important to notice that it tends to orientalize and attack the "yellow" race. Somehow the Asian heritage of Latin America, because of its shorter history, was contemplated by Vasconcelos as the less "cosmic."

[38] Banton, *Racial Theories,* 76.

[39] In other words, the direct connection between Latin American history and reproduction in *La raza cósmica* completely obliterates the politics of the reproductive subjects and their historicity. To my knowledge, there is presently no feminist reading of *La raza cósmica,* although Sylvia Molloy has developed an insightful critique of Vasconcelos's autobiography and its relation to the mother figure; see Sylvia Molloy, "Memory, Lineage, and Representation," *At Face Value: Autobiographical Writing in Spanish America* (Cambridge: Cambridge University Press, 1991), 137-208.

[40] Jean Franco, "Memoria, narración y repetición: la narrativa hispanoamericana en la época de la cultura de masas," *Más allá del boom: Literatura y mercado*, ed. David Viñas, Angel Rama, et al. (Mexico City: Marcha Editores, 1981), 111-29. See also Peter Earl, "Utopia," 150-51.

[41] Vasconcelos, *La raza cósmica*, 277.

[42] Molloy, "Memory," 206.

[43] Martínez-Echazábal, "Positivismo," 129; my translation.

[44] Paz, *Labyrinth*, 155.

[45] To follow the new articulations between race and politics in contemporary Latin America, see the discussion of Brazil's case in Howard Winant, "'The Other Side of the Process': Racial Formation in Contemporary Brazil," *On Edge*, ed. Yúdice et al., 85-113.

[46] García-Canclini, *Culturas híbridas*; Homi K. Bhabha, *The Location of Culture* (New York: Routledge, 1994).

[47] To see a well-intentioned but neoliberal actualization of Vasconcelos's project, see Leopoldo Zea "Vasconcelos y la utopía de la raza cósmica," *Cuadernos Americanos* 7.37 (January-February 1993): 23-36.

[48] Didier T. Jaén, "Introduction" in José Vasconcelos, *La raza cósmica* (Los Angeles: Centro de Publicaciones, 1979), xxxi. In this 1997 edition, see p. xxix.

BIBLIOGRAPHY

I. Works by Vasconcelos (first editions):

—*Teoría dinámica del derecho*. México, 1907.

—*Gabino Barreda y las ideas contemporáneas*. México, 1910.

—*Pitágoras: una teoría del ritmo*. Havana, 1916.

—*La intelectualidad mexicana* (conferencia). México, 1916.

—*El monismo estético: ensayos*. México, 1918.

—*Divagaciones literarias*. México, 1919.

—*Artículos*. San José, Costa Rica, 1920.

—*Prometeo vencedor*. México, 1920.

—*La caída de Carranza: de la dictadura a la libertad*. México, 1920.

—*Estudios indostánicos*. México, 1920.

—*Orientaciones del pensamiento en México*. Córdoba, Argentina, 1922.

—*Ideario de acción*. Lima, Perú, 1924.

—*La revulsión de la energía*. México, 1924.

—*Los últimos cincuenta años*. México, 1924.

—*La raza cósmica*. Barcelona, 1925.

—*Indología*. Paris, 1926.

—*Aspects of Mexican Civilization*. Chicago, 1927.

119

—*Tratado de metafísica.* México, 1929.   *

—*Pesimismo alegre.* Madrid, 1931.

—*Ética.* Madrid, 1932.

—*La sonata mágica.* Madrid, 1933.

—*Hispanoamérica frente a los nacionalismos agresivos de Europa y los Estados Unidos.* La Plata, 1934

—*Carta a la intelectualidad mexicana.* México, 1934.

—*Bolivarismo y Monroísmo.* Santiago de Chile, 1934.

—*De Robinsón a Odiseo.* Madrid, 1935.

—*Estética.* México, 1935.

—*Ulises criollo.* México, 1935.

—*La tormenta.* México: Botas, 1936.

—*Qué es el comunismo?* México, 1936.

—*Qué es la Revolución?* México: Botas, 1937.

—*Historia del pensamiento filosófico.* México, 1937.

—*Breve historia de México.* México, 1937.

—*El desastre.* México, 1938.

—*El proconsulado.* México, 1939.

—*Simón Bolívar.* México, 1939.

—*Manual de Filosofía.* México, 1940.

—*Páginas escogidas.* México, 1940.

—*Hernán Cortés, creador de la nacionalidad.* México, 1941.

—*Vasconcelos.* México, Secretaría de Educación Pública, 1942.

—*Apuntes para la historia de México.* México, 1943.

—*El realismo científico.* México, 1943.

—*La idea franciscana de la conquista de América.* México, 1943

—*El viento de Bagdad.* México, 1945.

—*Lógica orgánica.* México, 1945.

—*La cita.* México, 1945.

—*Los robachicos.* México, 1946.

—*Discursos (1920-1950).* México: Ediciones Botas, 1950.

—*Todología: filosofía de la coordinación.* México, 1952.

—*Filosofía estética.* Buenos Aires, 1952.

—*Temas contemporáneos.* México, 1956.

—*En el ocaso de mi vida.* México, 1957.

—*Obras completas.* México, 1957-1961.

—*Don Evaristo Madero.* México, 1958.

—*Cartas políticas.* México, 1959.

—*La flama.* México, 1959.

—*Letanías del atardecer.* México, 1959.

—*Ulises criollo.* Ed. Ronald Hilton. Boston: Heath, 1960.

—*A Mexican Ulysses: The Autobiography of José Vasconcelos.* Translated and edited by William Rex Crawford. Bloomington: Indiana University Press, 1963.

II. Works on Vasconcelos (selected):

Ahumada, Herminio. *Los fundamentos sociológicos de la raza síntesis: Lester F. Ward y José Vasconcelos.* México: Juan Pablos, 1930.

—*José Vasconcelos: una vida que iguala con la acción el pensamiento.* México: Botas, 1937.

Ahumada, Rodolfo. "The Philosophies of Antonio Caso y José Vasconcelos with Special Emphasis on Their Concepts of Value." Diss., University of Southern California, 1963.

Alessio Robles, Vito. *Mis andanzas con nuestro Ulises.* México: Botas, 1938.

Arce, David N. *Bibliografía de José Vasconcelos.* México: Biblioteca Nacional, 1958.

Bar-Lewaw, Itzhak. *Introducción crítico-bibliográfica a José Vasconcelos (1882-1959).* Madrid: Ediciones Latino-americanas, 1965.

—*José Vasconcelos: vida y obra.* México: Clásica Selecta Editora Librera, 1965.

—"El mundo literario de José Vasconcelos." *Actas del III Congreso Internacional de Hispanistas,* México, 1968, 97-103.

Basave Fernández del Valle, Agustín. *La filosofía de José Vasconcelos (el hombre y su sistema).* Madrid: Ediciones Cultura Hispánica, 1958.

—"El destino de José Vasconcelos." *Revista mexicana de filosofía*, Vol. III, no. 3 (1959), 27-31.

Bonifaz Nuño, Rubén. "Imagen de Vasconcelos." *Abside*, Vol. XXVIII, 79-81.

Brightman, Edgar Sheffield. "Discussion: Don José Vasconcelos." *Philosophy and Phenomenological Research*, Vol. 7 (1946-47), 453-460.

Carreras, Francisco J. *José Vasconcelos: filosofía de la coordinación*. Madrid: Anaya, 1970.

Carrión, Benjamín. *Los creadores de la nueva América: José Vasconcelos, Manuel Ugarte, F. García Calderón, Alcides Arguedas*. Prólogo de Gabriela Mistral. Madrid: Sociedad general española de librería, 1928.

Caso, Antonio. "Estudios indostánicos, por José Vasconcelos." *Discursos a la nación mexicana*. México: Porrúa, 1922.

Castro Leal, Antonio. "Ante el féretro de Vasconcelos." *Abside*, Vol. XXIII, 353-357.

Corro Vina, J. Manuel. *Andrew Almafán, la reconstrucción de México y el crimen del vasconcelismo*. Corpus Christi, Texas: "El Puerto," 1930.

Cotte-Thorner, Guillermo. "Germen novelístico en Vasconcelos." *La Nueva Democracia*, Vol.XXXVI, ii, 32-35.

De Beer, Gabriella. "José Vasconcelos and His Social Thought." Diss., Columbia. *DA*, 26:6 (May-June 1966), 7313-7314.

—*José Vasconcelos and His World*. New York: Las Americas, 1966.

—"José Vasconcelos vis-á-vis the United States." *Revista Interamericana de Bibliografía*, Vol. 17 (1967), 414-430.

Guandique, J. S. "De Gavidia a Masferrer hasta Vasconcelos." *Abside,* Vol. 32 (1968), 459-472.

Guisa y Azevedo, Jesús. *Me lo dijo Vasconcelos.* México: Polis, 1965.

Guy, Alain. "José Vasconcelos et Bergson." *Revista mexicana de filosofía,* Vol. II, no. 3 (1959), 63-70.

Haddox, John H. "José Vasconcelos: Mexican Philosopher." *The Personalist,* Vol. XLIII (1962), 453-465.

—"The Aesthetic Philosophy of José Vasconcelos." *International Philosophical Quarterly,* Vol. IV (1964), 283-296.

—*Vasconcelos of Mexico, Philosopher and Prophet.* Austin: University of Texas Press, 1967.

Hilton, Ronald. "José Vasconcelos." *The Americas,* Vol. VII, 395-412.

Homenaje del Colegio Nacional a Samuel Ramos y José Vasconcelos. México: Edit. del Colegio Nacional, 1960.

Instituto Nacional de Bellas Artes. Departamento de Literatura. *En la muerte de José Vasconcelos: 7 oraciones fúnebres.* México, 1959.

Jaén, Didier T. *"La raza cósmica* de Vasconcelos: una re-evaluación" *Texto Crítico,* vol. I, núm. 1 (enero-junio, 1975), 14-21.

Juárez, Nicandro Francisco. "José Vasconcelos' Theory of the Cosmic Race." MA Thesis, University of California, Los Angeles, 1965.

Junco, Alfonso. "Vasconcelos íntimo." *Abside,* Vol. XXIV, 373-377.

Magdalena, Mauricio. *Las palabras perdidas*. México: Fondo de Cultura Económica, 1956.

Mantero, Manuel. "Vasconcelos o la filosofía como vida." *Estudios Americanos*, Vol. XVIII (1959), 261-267.

Martínez, José Luis. "La obra literaria de José Vasconcelos."*Literatura Mexicana Siglo XX*. México, 1949, 265-279.

McDonald, James K. "Motivos autóctonos en el pensamiento ensayístico de México en el siglo XX." Diss., University of California, Berkeley. *DA*, I 30:4459A.

Millán, María del Carmen. "La Generación del Ateneo y el ensayo mexicano." *Nueva Revista de Filología Hispánica*, Vol. XV (1961), 625-636.

Nicotra di Leopoldo, G. *Pensamientos inéditos de José Vasconcelos*. México: Botas, 1970.

Pani, Alberto J. *Mi contribución al nuevo régimen (1910-1933) (A propósito del "Ulises Criollo," autobiografía del licenciado, don José Vasconcelos)*. México: Cultura, 1936.

Pérez, Ismael Diego. "Vasconcelos o el pensamiento ibero-americano," *Revista Mexicana de filosofía*, Vol. II, no. 3 (1959), 47-61.

Phillips, Richard Baker. "José Vasconcelos and the Mexican Revolution of 1910." Diss., Stanford 1954, *DA*, 14:1 (1954), 347-348.

Prieto, José María. "Balance del pensamiento de José Vasconcelos." *Estudios Americanos*, Vol. XVIII (1959), 269-275.

Robles, Oswaldo. "José Vasconcelos, el filósofo de la emoción creadora." *Filosofía y Letras*, Vol. XIII (1947), 211-225.

— "José Vasconcelos." *Revista mexicana de filosofía,* Vol. II, no. 3 (1959), 9-17.

Romanell, Patrick. "Bergson en México: un tributo a José Vasconcelos." *Humanitas,* I, 1, 265-266.

— "Il monismo estético di José Vasconcelos." *Rivista di Filosofía Moderna,* Vol. XLIV (1956), 137-157.

Sacoto, Antonio. "Aspectos indigenistas en la obra literaria de José Vasconcelos." *Cuadernos Americanos,* 163:151-157.

Sánchez, Luis Alberto. "El Vasconcelos que conozco." *Nueva Democracia,* Vol. XL, no. IV (196), 45-47.

Sánchez Villaseñor, José. " 'El Pitágoras' y los orígenes del pensamiento estético vasconcelista." *Revista mexicana de filosofía,* Vol. II, no. 3 (1959), 19-25.

Skirius, John. *José Vasconcelos y la cruzada de 1929* (México: Siglo XXI), 1978.

— "Vasconcelos and México de Afuera (1928)" *Aztlán, International Journal of Chicano Research,* vol. 7, num. 3 (Fall 1976) pp. 479-496.

— "La odisea de Vasconcelos". *Vuelta,* vol. I, núm. 7 (Junio, 1977) pp. 29-32.

Valenzuela, Alberto. "Madero en Vasconcelos y Huerta en García Naranjo." *Abside,* Vol. XXII (1958), 480-489.

Villegas, Abelardo. "José Vasconcelos." *Filosofía de lo mexicano,* México, 1960, pp. 65-99.

Vita, Luis Washington. "José Vasconcelos (1882-1959). *Revista mexicana de filosofía,* Vol. II, no. 3 (1959), 71-75.